The Charmer's Root: Witching Ways with Common Flora

Copyright © 2024 by Roger J. Horne. All rights reserved. First Edition.

No part of this book may be used or reproduced in any manner whatsoever without the prior written permission of the copyright holder. The formulas and recipes in this book are not intended as a substitute for medical guidance. Consult with your doctor before working with any plant.

ISBN 978-1-7367625-6-1

Moon over the Mountain Press

The Charmer's Root

Witching Ways with Common Flora

Roger J. Horne

Also by Roger J. Horne:

Folk Witchcraft: A Guide to Lore, Land, & the Familiar Spirit for the Solitary Practitioner

The Witch's Art of Incantation: Spoken Charms, Spells, & Curses in Folk Witchcraft

A Broom at Midnight: Thirteen Gates of Witchcraft by Spirit Flight

Cartomancy in Folk Witchcraft: Playing Cards and Marseille Tarot in Divination, Magic, & Lore

The Witches' Devil: Myth and Lore for Modern Cunning

Contents

Introduction 1

Part One: Witching Ways

Magical Herbalism in Folk Witchery 9
Seeking Green Spirits 22
The Language of Growing Things 36
Conjuring the Green Spirit 53
Occult Botanical Keys and Maps 76
Charming with Herbs 85
Riding Plants 101

Part Two: Recipes

A Note of Caution 115
Preparing Herbs 116
Infusions 118
Essences 120
Tinctures 123
Vinegars 125
Oils 127
Ointments, Salves, and Balms 129
Powders 132

Salts 133
Incense 135
Inks 138
Talismans 140
Dollies and Roots 144
Plant Spirit Water 146

Part Three: Common Flora

Agrimony 156
Archangel 158
Bitter Dock 160
Bittersweet Nightshade 163
Black Nightshade 166
Burdock 169
Buttercup 171
Catnip 173
Chickweed 175
Chicory 177
Cinquefoil 179
Clover 181
Dandelion 185
Fleabane 188
Groundsel 190
Heather 193
Henbane 196

Honeysuckle	199
Lemon Balm	202
Mallow	204
Mint	206
Mugwort	208
Mullein	211
Plantain	213
Prickly Lettuce	216
Ragwort	218
Shepherd's Purse	221
Solomon's Seal	223
Sow Thistle	226
Star of Bethlehem	229
Teasel	231
Thistle	233
Thornapple	235
Violet	238
Wood Sorrel	241
Wormwood	244
A Further Index of Plant Associations	247
Epilogue: The Black Meadow	257

Introduction

When we step into the wild, we step into a world of spirits. Whether it be the woods, the mossy creek bed, or simply an open field near our home, we stand in the presence of ancient magical beings. The wild cleavers catch and grasp us with their hairy leaves. The black nightshade sings out with its unruly mixture of dark berries and pale, delicate flowers. The wild is not a gentle, idyllic place, but is barbed and messy, its teeth sharp, guarding its treasures.

It is no wonder then that charmers throughout the ages—from our ancestors hundreds of years ago, to you and I in these modern times—feel eyes upon us in wild places. We are not alone. And it is in that knowledge that we are compelled to tread lightly, carefully, tenderly—to learn the language of the honeysuckle and clover, to observe carefully what patterns and instincts lie within their natures and how these elements lend potency to the art of witchcraft.

Nor are we merely observers in the wilderness; at our touch, the ferns curl and close. Our footsteps shake loose the spores of fungi, that they might spread and grow, forming their invisible network of pale tendrils in the soil. We are participants in the wild, but we are not its protagonists. We are not the center of creation any more than the serpent or the toad. This, too, is a kind of wisdom.

If we are careful students, if we can put aside our modern impulse to view the living forest as made of mere "things," mere objects of use, then there are greater treasures to be gained here, for as charmers and witches have known for quite a long time, these living beings are not asleep, but awake. Their vitality is unlike ours, but in no way lesser. They are possessed of spirits that can dispose blessings and curses as they wish, and their wisdom and friendship, though hard won, are the most potent gifts the green world can offer to our kind.

The focus of this book is the magical folklore and wisdom of common flora, which is to say, the plants we encounter in everyday life. While there is great joy and reward to be found in procuring and growing rare and exotic plants for magical use, we often overlook the everyday plants growing in places of nearby wilderness—in countryside thickets, sprawling fields, and overgrown cemeteries. The herbs that thrive in these places are just as ancient and magical as any rare species we can order over the internet, and often even more so.

If anything, the proliferation of these old, wise beings is a testament to their potency: they thrive and spread, humming with vitality, eager to meet us on our walk through the woods or stroll through the field, bursting forth through cracks in pavement and reaching out to us in city parks and wild meadows. Instead of answering this call to meet and learn from these spirits, we often ignore them, throwing their offerings of wisdom and power away with both hands, which is a waste and a loss, for their magic is rich indeed, and we are left disconnected from the living land around us.

These plants have the added benefit for us of being available where we live in their full life cycle. They grow wild, and usually need no gardener to tend them. We can simply walk out the door and witness for ourselves their natures—where they grow, how they proliferate, what their stages of maturity look like. This is valuable information, for it allows us to form a relationship with the plant that is personal and grounded, and these keys to their physical development translate easily into magical keys unlocking their power in our craft.

Strictly speaking, not all of the plants that witches may work with in their various locales are "officially" categorized as herbs. The plants most call herbs are usually given this categorization due to their use in flavoring food or providing medicine. Loosely, we can think of the "herb" as being a wanted plant, while the "weed" has traditionally been defined as an unwanted one. Folk witches like myself, though, might argue that all plants possess some form of *spiritual* medicine, even if they are not edible or medicinal on a biochemical level. It is the plant spirit itself that supplies its magical potencies, which can be safely conjured even from toxic plants via methods that are ritualistic in nature, requiring no ingestion or even skin contact with the plant's physical body. Approached this way, every plant becomes sacred, and we are able to find safe ways of working with our local flora, connecting with the land beneath our own two feet.

To be sure, this work will be likewise valuable when working with certain rarer plants important to the legacy of traditional witchcraft, including those legendary nightshades of old, but our real focus is on the plants commonly available to witches in the soils of North America, the British Isles, and some other regions of a similar climate. Honestly, though, if you live in an area that experiences freezing temperatures in the winter, most of these plants will most likely be present where you live—simply because these common plants have spread throughout the world over many centuries. Still, a book focused on common magical plants simply must have a regionally defined scope, and its author, being simply another witch and not an all-knowing entity, must admit the limitations of his experience and knowledge. I'm simply another practitioner on this crooked path, and I cannot speak to the unique flora of lands I have not walked. We can only write what we know, in the end. Still, I believe the magical methods and approaches shared here will be of use to witches working with a variety of plants, wherever they may be.

The first part of this book describes a series of reliable approaches and techniques. These are aimed at identifying plants, studying them for indications of their natures and their potencies, researching their folklore, forging relationships with plant spirits, conjuring the spirit of the plant, achieving spirit flight with the aid of plant spirits, and performing herbal charms to usher in desired change. The second part of this book consists of recipes for herbal preparations. The third part is a folkloric materia magica—a series of folk-magical entries on some of the most common plants in the British Isles and North America. Unlike most herbals, the focus of these entries is on the folklore and mythology surrounding these historic plants rather than their medicinal use—in addition to my own interpretation of their magical signatures.

Part of the joy of the green charming arts is learning for oneself the personality of our local flora, experiencing first-hand what their physical and spiritual presence feels like. I hope this book will serve as a point of initiation for your own personal practice, dear reader. Witchcraft is both embodied and ensouled; it is a thing we do and a thing we become. Feel out for yourself how these ancient beings influence your own craft. Befriend them. Form your own alliances with these mighty spirits. Find a witching way that is yours and yours alone. Let this work be like a trail map, hand-written, passed from one witch to another—in the full knowledge that new notes will be etched in its margins, names will be overwritten and rewritten, new keys and secrets will be scrawled over old ones. This is how the old witchery has always been. This is how it remains alive, vital, and personal to each.

Part One:
Witching Ways

Magical Herbalism
in Folk Witchery

When Scottish charmer Bessie Dunlop was tried for witchcraft in the late 1500s, there were no accusations of cursing, magical torment, or other forms of *maleficium*, or malevolent craft. She was accused of consulting with spirits, making auguries and predictions, and, of course, casting magical charms with plants. It was the spirit world, she claimed, that taught her the magical use of a variety of plants, including licorice, ginger, clover, and others. None accused Bessie of doing harm, and in some cases, individuals readily testified that she helped her community with her craft. Bessie Dunlop had provided magical services to aid several poor neighbors, usually in exchange for food or other simple trades. She had also been employed by members of the aristocracy, though she did not appear to profit monetarily from her work. She was ultimately executed, the fate of roughly 1,500 accused witches in early modern Scotland, two thirds being women. Bessie would have probably described herself simply as a seer, healer, or charmer, but it is the word *witchcraft* that was used to condemn her.

Today, many folk charmers like myself have embraced the word *witch*, sometimes with caveats or explanation, but always with the goal of resisting the villainization of our inherited folk-magical traditions. The folkways that make up the very real traditions of witchcraft come to us from older times, having roots in the paganism and animism practiced by our ancient ancestors, people with less technology and fewer modern luxuries who spent a great deal of time learning the popular wisdom, superstitions, and uses of their local flora. While texts like the *Compendium Maleficarum* (and even later works like *The Witch-Cult in Western Europe*) seek to suggest that witchcraft existed as a unified, cohesive, organized body of members, the truth is messier than this, for the narrative of the witch actually villainized a great variety of practices in many different folk traditions, binding together all of these currents of occult praxis in the single word *witch*.

The association of witches with magical herbalism is both historic and folkloric. Preserved manuals of historic magic, such as the *Lacnunga*, *The Grimorium Verum*, *The Heptameron*, and many others contain records of the magical uses of plants by charmers in previous eras. Even the *Carmina Gadelica*, a famous collection of old Scottish incantations, contains charms designed to conjure the magical potencies of common plants like ragwort, primrose, and juniper. The *Compendium Maleficarum* of the 1600s famously villainized the herbal arts of the folk charmer with incendiary passages like the following:

> The poisons used by witches are compounded and mixed from many sorts of poisons, such as the leaves and stalks and roots of plants; from animals, fishes, venomous reptiles, stones and metals; sometimes these are reduced to powder and sometimes to an ointment.

While the poisoner's craft is quite real and requires a profound knowledge of herbalism, passages like the one above were also used to stir up loathing for practitioners of the herbal arts generally, to cast doubt on the motives of a community's healers and to sow the seeds of fear.

This fear would have served a distinct purpose, allowing witch hunters to grow their business and make names for themselves as they traveled from town to town, collecting their payment and hanging innocent people. Their victims were usually not even practitioners of any charming arts whatsoever, but were simply disliked people who made easy targets. This fact would have made little difference to terrified communities who were convinced by self-proclaimed "experts" that their town was under siege by the forces of evil. Even church officials in the early modern era expressed horror at the chaos wrought by witch hunters. The occasional prosecution of an actual charmer was, to many church officials, not worth the carnage. Interestingly, some charmers and cunning folk evolved their practice during the witch hunts, offering divinatory services to help locate witches and even selling protective magical charms to keep witches at bay. Some proclaimed themselves "white witches"—even while offering deadly curse-work to their clients. While it would be easy to judge their choices, we should look on these charmers with compassion, for it is difficult for us to imagine the fear they would have felt for the lives of their loved ones—even their children—if they did not side with popular movement growing around them.

Within every image of the witch disseminated in popular culture, there hides a kernel of truth. Behind the popular image of the hag stirring her cauldron lies the old folk healer, cunning woman, and midwife who used local plants to prepare magical formulas for sale or trade. Behind the terror of the witch's curse lie the old folk-magical traditions of cursing, which were well-known and practiced in nearly every community. (Scottish cursing traditions are especially interesting here, for their performance evolved into the well-known poetic form of the *flyting*.) Behind the cackling witch astride her broom lies the folklore of faeries and human charmers who were able to cross between worlds in spirit form, sometimes by "riding" plants—a practice that is neither imaginary nor lost today, but merely veiled behind superstitions and "old wives' tales." Behind the famous image of the screaming mandrake root lies a great wealth of charms to do with the roots of various plants, sometimes fashioned into simulacra or poppets (as with mandrake), but also kept as spirit vessels and fetishes for many purposes, often to honor the spirit of a plant itself in a kind of dried and preserved relic.

Witchcraft is now more popular than ever, and includes a variety of traditions that co-exist and sometimes mingle, like creek beds coming together in a river. This tapestry includes traditional witchcraft, shaped by famed modern witches like Robert Cochrane and Andrew Chumbley, Feri witchcraft, founded by Cora and Victor Anderson, the modern religion of Wicca, established by Gerald Gardner, and, of course, the smattering of outlying, non-mainstream traditions that we call folk witchery (which are sometimes included in definitions of traditional craft and sometimes not, depending on who is speaking).

It is this last branch that best describes my own craft. For folk witches, our charms and traditions are deeply personal, shaped by our cultural heritage, our ancestors, and the plants, animals, stones, and creeks of the land around us. The old superstitions, lore, grimoires, and folk charms are, for us, our trove of magical knowledge. My ancestors practiced charming in the traditions of Appalachian herb doctoring and Scottish cunning craft (sometimes called skilly craft), so it is these currents that shape most of the craft I perform, but there are so many other branches of what we call "folk witchcraft" that it is impossible to name them all. Practitioners of faery doctoring, pow-wow, brujeria, pellar work, hoodoo, stregoneria, and many forms of magical folk-Catholicism—all equally vital, living folk traditions—often choose to identify under the umbrella term of "folk witchery." It is not only possible, but quite likely that you, dear reader, have an ancestor or two who utilized the folk charming arts in some capacity. It is not as uncommon as most people think.

And it is not only likely, but almost certain that at least one of your ancestors, dear reader, has practiced charming with plants. The association of the herbal arts with magic and witchcraft is an ancient one that seems to occur in the folklore of nearly every region on earth. In ancient Greece, the term *pharmakeia* referred to herbalism, the poisoner's arts, and practical witchcraft together at once, and one wonders whether the observance of patterns of meaning in local flora was, in some ways, the "root" of humankind's earliest magical arts. After all, it was our skill at discerning the properties at work in plants and our ability to categorize and read these signs that led to not only the development of early medicines and agriculture, but quite likely the development of our earliest magics as well.

Just as certain plants have long been used to treat a variety of medical conditions, they have also been used to treat spiritual ones—correcting imbalances, bringing luck, protecting against harm, and even bringing justice to those who wrong us. The old herbalists, hundreds of years ago, analyzed plants for their "signatures," deducing planetary influences and medical uses. (Their theories were sometimes wrong, of course, but let us at least admit that most of us would not be here if the old herbalists had not treated and cured one of our ancestors.) Similarly, witches analyze the spirit that animates a plant, deducing its personality, its magical potencies, and the means to awaken its power in the act of ritual.

Too often, magical herbalism is reduced to tables of correspondences, often with little or no explanation as to why an herb like thistle is ruled by Mars or why chicory is ruled by the Sun. While correspondences can be helpful in our craft, we must be willing to admit a simple truth here: calling to a plant spirit we do not know very well is unlikely to illicit a strong response. It's not unlike asking a favor from a mere acquaintance. They might be willing to aid us, but only to a point, for we haven't formed a bond with them, allowing them to know us and for us to know them in turn. Just like working with the spirits of the grimoires or the deities of the ancients, we will be more effective in our art if we spend a little more time getting to know them intimately, learning their lore, their various names, their interactions with charmers over the centuries, watching how they grow and thrive in the world around us, and conjuring their spirits by inviting them into our presence. Even if we cannot find a particular plant where we live, we can at least learn its folklore and history of use in order to better understand its relationship with humans across the ages.

In the process of understanding the stories of ancient plants, we run into an interesting dilemma: that medical and magical usage are somewhat entangled. Parsing medical herbalism from magical herbalism is a tricky business, for the two are, in many ways, intertwined, but this distinction is necessary, for our true focus is not the study of a given plant's effects on the body as verified by the scientific method, but rather, the effects of interacting with the potent spirit of the plant in a ritual setting. This work is no less complex or demanding, but we must admit that it is different. Magical herbalism seeks out spiritual truths rather than scientific ones, and these truths arrive in the form of spiritual revelation and personal transformation, not the hard data of the botanist's work.

And yet, we nonetheless find places of overlap, in part owing to the history of herbalism itself. For example, Culpeper's *Complete Herbal*, written in the 1600s, describes the herb chickweed as being under the dominion of the Moon due to its ability to cool and soothe inflammation, a purpose for which it is used in salves to this very day. The spirit of the herb bears this same hallmark; its nature is watery, nurturing, and usually friendly to the practitioner. We probably would not drop the juice of the chickweed into our eye to soothe redness, as Culpeper recommended in his time, for we have a variety of more thoroughly sanitized medicines available for this purpose that don't carry the risk of infection. We might, however, use an oil of chickweed to anoint a candle when connecting with lunar currents in our craft. Better yet, we might prepare a sachet, a type of talisman containing the dried herb, in order to usher in a happy beginning of a new endeavor, since this plant spirit is associated with renewal due to its early emergence in the spring.

By paying close attention to the behavior of a particular plant, we are able to deduce its properties in a way that is similar to the old herbalists, but also distinct. The principle behind this method is sometimes called the *doctrine of signatures*, which suggests that the appearance and behavior of a plant conveys its properties and uses. In a most literal sense, the old herbalists sometimes looked to a plant resembling a part of the body that it might be used to treat. Often, though, the qualities of plants were analyzed along different lines: planetary rulers, zodiacal influences, elemental properties, and other magical and alchemical categories. For magical purposes, a planetary analysis of a given plant is more than sufficient as a starting point, for it often yields surprisingly complex results. A given herb may have as many as five planetary influences, determined by certain hallmarks in its physical nature, the history of its use, and of course, its folklore.

Magical herbalism in folk witchery tends to be a hands-on, messy, experiential learning process. While it is sometimes necessary to purchase dried herbs from afar, we must still take the time to call to the plant spirit, to consecrate what has been desecrated in the machinery of production and shipping, to "hallow the leaves" once again so that the spirit within them remembers its own potency and answers to our call. In our age of convenience, we tend to value efficiency over potency, but this value system conflicts with the heart of our craft. Much like tasting a stew to determine when it is "right," a magical charm that is well-wrought leaves us with a certain feeling that is difficult to describe in words. This sense of satisfaction usually comes from work that is slowly savored, fully felt, and patiently performed, like the unguent that is carefully heated, mixed with beeswax, and allowed to cool, its magical potency taking shape as surely as its substance firms and solidifies, or like the spirit seal drawn in flour or cornstarch, a symbol derived from visions and dreams of the plant spirit, now realized in the world, welcomed with incense and old words of conjuration. The potent charm can appear quite simple, like calling to the plant spirit while holding its root in the hand, but behind this deceptively simple appearance lies a mountain of unseen labor, for the witch has spent time and effort learning the folklore of the plant, observing the patterns woven into its living body, discerning the personality at work behind its nature, and acquiring or developing the spoken charm that will awaken the spirit—all of this work comes in addition to the mere task of harvesting and drying the root that is its chthonic (or underworld-dwelling) body.

The rewards of this work, however, are immense. We can craft our own fumigations in the form of herb bundles or magically-imbued incense cones, herb-infused oils to dress talismans, candles, and even our bodies, powders to sprinkle or blow upon property, vessels to call in the presence of a spirit to a place as its guardian, plant-derived inks to create sigils and spiritual pacts, sachets and other talismans to be worn or placed in order to call in the plant spirit's influence, not to mention plant spirit water, flower essences, and infused vinegars used to dress doorways, belongings, or property lines. More importantly, we can connect with these spirits as magical allies in our craft, friends and neighbors to rely on, allies who will teach us and help us grow strong in our arts. The limitations of magical herbalism are only as far-reaching as our skill and dedication, for the spirits living within these plants are ancient and powerful, revered across the ages, and they have aided charmers like ourselves for centuries.

I would like to take a moment to share some warnings here, reader, because I do care about your safety. Be mindful while working with the recipes and plants in this book that not all herbs are safe for everyone to touch, smell, burn, or consume. While it is perhaps obvious that poisonous plants like deadly nightshade, thornapple, and henbane carry lethal danger, we can easily harm ourselves by working with any plant before understanding how it affects our body as an individual. It is recommended that any practitioner consult with a physician in order to determine any possible danger to oneself due to allergies, sensitivities, medical conditions, or pregnancy before working with a plant via touch, ingestion, inhalation, or by any other method. Rely on guidance from a medical professional as well as your good common sense to protect your own health and the health of any loved ones, human or animal, who may be exposed to a plant in the process. In addition, we must be careful about where we source our plants, for even the most edible herbs can grow where pesticides, herbicides, and pollutants have been sprayed, forever altering the chemical composition of the plant and sometimes rendering it dangerous. This is to say nothing of the danger of misidentifying plants, which is quite serious. Many plants are almost indistinguishable from poisonous look-alikes. One should always be certain that the correct herb is being used, and I highly recommend consulting a trained herbalist or botanist to help with the identification process.

Thankfully, we need not expose ourselves to dangerous toxins in order to work with a plant's spiritual potencies. Because this work involves calling to the plant's spirit and not utilizing biochemical effects from its body, we actually *do not need to touch the plant in order to call on its magic.* The second section of this book provides alternative recipes that allow us to work with potentially poisonous plants in a safe way via the folk-magical principle of contagion and the old folk practice of spiritual exchange. If your health prevents you from handling or ingesting a particular plant, do consider using these alternative formulae instead.

Lastly, though not of least importance, I would like to take a moment to encourage you to be good to yourself on this path. Magical herbalism is often an entry point through which new witches arrive at their own lasting practice. If this describes you, dear reader, please be kind to yourself while embarking on this path. Be patient with yourself. Allow yourself to explore and experiment as you work through the material in this book and others. If working with a particular charm or spirits brings up psychological pain due to previous religious trauma or for any other reason, slow down, and take a breath. Witchcraft is not an easy path, nor is it right for everyone.

In fact, it is still necessary, in many parts of the world today, to be selective when sharing with others your interest in witchcraft. The fearful carnage of the witch hunts is not entirely gone, but lingers in many rural areas where religious zealotry has taken root, in churches that see "evil" everywhere and are eager to label those of different cultures and faiths as enemies. (Ironically, it is also in rural places where some of our oldest treasures of witchery survive, preserved in lore and superstition.)

Whether you choose to call yourself a witch, a charmer, a healer, or any other term, I invite you to consider yourself a part of this body of living traditions. Be good to yourself, and work in the knowledge that many, many charmers came before you. No facet of this craft is new, for some sorcerous wise one from before has surely worked any charm you may attempt. Those echoes of the old conjurers are all around us, offering us both humility and comfort. We are humbled by the preserved lore that precedes us; we find comfort in the long line of charmers who came before.

Seeking Green Spirits

The spirits of plants have a great deal to teach us. On a practical level, plant spirits can offer magical keys in the form of sigils revealed through visions, incantations revealed in a whisper, and clues to hidden magical techniques through subtle suggestions. On a deeper level, plant spirits can teach us to live well and to better understand ourselves. Their wisdom is ingrained in their natures, a balm of simplicity against the mental and emotional suffering that spreads like a plague in our information age. The compass plant, or prickly lettuce, twists its leaves to follow the sun as the day progresses, reminding us that we, too, must bend to follow that which nourishes us. The seeds of the thornapple, or jimsonweed, fall freely from the dried and opened pods in the fall so that they may be tempered by the ice and cold, rendered ready to germinate in the spring. We sorcerous folk are quite the same, for the various "winters" of our lives do not break us, but merely cause little cracks and fissures in the husk we wear about the spirit, awakening the slumbering magic within. Indeed, the oldest charming arts are born of the traditions of poor, common folk, who often suffered at the hands of the wealthy and powerful. Suffering, for witching folk, can stimulate new gifts that bloom in time.

Nor do most plant spirits thrive in isolation; the otherworld, just like this one, is actually a complex ecosystem of beings that are interdependent and full of intentionality. While some spiritual traditions seek to define all spirits as "good" or "evil," "angels" or "demons," the truth is more complex than any simple binary. All spirits have a personality, a complex inner nature, and like the living creatures of a forest, marsh, or ocean, they each have some important work to do, even if we do not always understand it. It is often said that fungi feast upon the dead, which is true, but it is also true that most plants rely on fungi in order to develop healthy root systems. This symbiotic relationship allows the plant's roots to stretch as the fungus tunnels its hair-like paths through soil. Like our green neighbors, we are more connected in the dark, unseen world than we imagine ourselves to be, nourishing one another and communicating without words. Magic, in part, occurs through this interdependence. As we begin studying the particularities of the plants on our own land, we should keep this important lesson in mind: we are, in some ways, already in kinship with these beings, and our work should honor and respect this relationship.

The arts of working with plant spirits—which have thankfully grown more popular in recent years—are not new, but old. The spirit of the elder tree is described in the old folklore as a woman, sometimes phrased the "elder mother" in the lore of northern Europe, sometimes as the "elder witch" in England. The common plantain is said to be the spirit of a young woman who wanders roadsides. The spirit of the violet is said to be a nymph who was hidden among the low foliage in order to evade a dangerous pursuer. The groundsel is sometimes referred to, in the British Isles and elsewhere, as an "old man," due to its white seedhead which goes bald. These plants—and all plants, if one looks closely enough—are not merely personified for our amusement, but in recognition of the fact that these beings have distinct *personalities.*

But the recognition of the plant spirit means something else as well: that the material of plants—their dried leaves, seeds, roots, flowers, and so forth—are actually vehicles for the *indwelling spirit*, which uses the physical body of the plant in order to act in the world. Seen through this lens, a jar of dried leaves or flowers is similar to the relics of saints housed in cathedrals across the world, for it uses preserved organic material as a corporeal connection to the ethereal spirit. Just as the enshrined finger or tooth of a saint brings the Catholic closer to the divine, so too does the root kept on the altar bring the witch closer to the power with which it is ensouled. For those who are new to this manner of craft, I recommend a simple ritual that we will simply call "hallowing the leaves." Its goal is quite straightforward: to quicken, perhaps only briefly and slightly, the spiritual potency preserved in dried plant matter. To do this, we will need to render sacred what was once desecrated by industry and manufacturing, to remind the plant of its spiritual nature, however forgotten and dormant its potency has become.

To Hallow the Leaves

Gather a plain, white candle and some dried herb with which you interact on a regular basis. This can be a simple cooking herb from a kitchen cabinet or an herb you have purchased in the past. It does not matter if it is new or quite old, but do choose an herb that is safe for you, noting your sensitivities, allergies, medical conditions, etc.

Spread a plain kitchen cloth on your counterspace, and set the candle beside it. Pour the dried herb into a new vessel, something that is not plastic. A ceramic or glass bowl does nicely. Set this bowl with the dried herb upon the cloth.

Light the candle slowly, with calm intention. Don't light it the way you would a cheap scented candle. Light it the way you would a taper at an altar. Remember that our goal is to draw the spirit out by honoring it with ritual.

Gather some of the dried herb into your hand. It doesn't need to be all of it. Try to look at its body the way you might look upon an animal slaughtered for food, or at the very least, gaze upon it the way you would a treasured antique that you have found tossed along the roadside. Look beyond what you see to what the plant might have been in its glorious maturity.

Speak to the herb, not with a booming, commanding voice, but with a gentle, kind one. The tone should feel intimate and encouraging, perhaps even a whisper. Later, we will explore more fully the use of historic incantations for calling to plant spirits, but for now, the words can be simple, perhaps something like the following, which is derived from early modern witch-lore and the calling of familiar spirits:

> *By and by, by and by,*
> *Come, thou spirit, by and by.*

Now, blow gently upon the herb in your hand. The goal is not to blow the herb all over the place, so the breath must be quite soft. Let just a bit of your breath mingle with the herb. Breath is a sacred tool, and we are, in effect, sharing a bit of our own magic with the plant spirit, just to give it enough strength in this moment that it can produce the tiniest nudge in return.

Close your eyes. Try not to focus on what you see or hear, but rather, what you *feel*. The herb in your hand may feel different than before, as if it now has more substance. You may feel a slight tingling in your hands, or you may simply feel a kind of *knowing* that is difficult to describe, much like the feeling when someone is looking at you, even if you cannot see them.

When you are finished, place the herb in a new vessel. Choose something worthy of a plant that is ensouled, perhaps a bottle, vial, or jar. Blow out the candle.

What you have hopefully experienced in the simple ritual above is a brief moment of encounter with a plant's spirit. You may or may not be aware of the plant's folklore, its magical associations, and its spiritual properties, but taking a moment to *feel* the spirit in the thing, to regard its body as something more than merely food or ornament, is like smiling at a stranger on the street. We've taken an initial step, and hopefully, we have felt some of the potency dwelling within this plant, whatever it may be. This is merely an exploratory exercise, though. Building a craft that incorporates the plants around us will require us to learn the personalities of these beings, to study their characters and their hidden powers.

The very best way to begin learning the magical potencies of plants is to look closely at the land around us and the plants that thrive where we live. This can feel difficult for those who did not grow up with someone around to help them identify common plants and the folklore and superstitions surrounding them. Thankfully, it is never too late to learn, and the process of scouting and identifying local plants is, simply put, a lot of fun. There is a simple joy in taking a walk around one's property or in a local park or cemetery, crouching over interesting plants, and taking notes or photographs to be identified later. Over the course of time, this process becomes a kind of game. How many plants can we identify by name? Having a friend or loved one join you in this activity is all the better. In the process, of course, we are mastering local flora, and we are beginning to recognize the green spirit neighbors who have been living nearby all along. This practice will, over time, become a source of power in our witchcraft.

The process of identifying local plants can feel daunting at first, but it is often surprising how many plants we already know by appearance. Most people can identify dandelion by its yellow flowers, round tuft of seeds, and jagged, tooth-like leaves. Thistle, too, stands out in the peak of summer with its tall purple blooms and thorny body. With a little practice, we can readily spot the gentle blue of the chicory growing in a field. Most of us know the familiar leaf pattern of a clover. In the spring, violets stand out easily with their bright purple, delicate flowers. If in doubt, begin with one or more of these or other plants you already know, and build from there.

If we encounter a plant that we cannot identify for certain, we can begin the process of identifying it via certain botanical cues. It is easiest to conduct this work with a flowering plant. (While there are varieties of plants that are non-flowering, such as ferns and mosses, let us set them aside for the moment, since the vast majority of plants bear blooms and seeds in order to reproduce.) Note, at the very least, the color of the flowers, the number of petals, and whether the leaves are opposite (that is, growing symmetrically along the left and right of the stem) or alternating (left, then right, then left again, going up the shoot). If the flower contains a furry-appearing disk in the center, such as a sunflower or daisy, we know already that it is most likely a member of the aster family. If the stem has a ridged, square appearance, we know it is probably a mint. Note the plant's appearance carefully, but be sure to also take a quick photograph for help with identification later.

With the image and description in hand, begin the process of identifying this plant. A good guide is helpful for this work, one of the more reliable books being Thomas J. Elpel's *Botany in a Day*. A good start can also be found on local university, agriculture, and botanical websites. Many of these types of sites provide "keys" which allow you to identify a plant by answering a series of questions about it via an online form. We are very fortunate in our information age to have one other powerful tool in our arsenal: the ability to search the web by image. Do be careful when using smartphone apps and reverse image searches, though. Since the results of this process are not always accurate, it is necessary to verify the results carefully to make sure the plant in question is not a poisonous look-a-like. Some plant identification apps are built and maintained in collaboration with trained botanists, so there's no reason to feel like one is "cheating" for using them if that is your preference. Keep in mind, though, that if you have any doubt at all about a plant's identity, it is best to consult with an expert to be certain before working with the plant. Queen Anne's lace, for example, looks very similar to hemlock, which can poison even by skin contact. You can always reach out, with your photograph as a reference point, to a local agricultural or botanical organization for expert help anytime you are unsure of a plant's species. Again, beginning with local university departments is a good start.

Modern witchcraft often prides itself on its flavor of resistance and rebellion, but in spite of this, there is a tendency for corporations to capitalize upon "witchy" products. If we are to form an herbal craft that is our own, connected to our actual life, our ancestors, and the natural world around us, we need to begin this work where we live. Don't let advertisers convince you that your craft is somehow incomplete without buying a plastic bag of dried plant matter shipped across the world. There is, of course, nothing wrong with experimenting with new plants, but remember that the world just outside of your door is quite literally overflowing with plants that are already living where you are, thriving, and eager to meet you and work with you in your craft. You do not need to pay for magical herbs in your craft, except perhaps with the currency of effort and patience. If you are living in an area that experiences freezing temperatures in the winter, then it is most likely that you can find plantain nearby, this plant being mentioned in magical tomes as early as the 10th century *Lacnunga*. Chicory, too, probably grows where you live, a magical plant in use since at least ancient Egypt. Even the most common culinary herbs have ancient uses in magic and superstition that are just as potent as any desiccated plant matter that can be bought online, more so if we grow them ourselves.

Many of the plants in this book, and the majority of the plants considered useful in witchcraft, have been called "weeds," a term often misinterpreted to mean a useless plant, one that has nothing to offer us and is therefore undesirable, a blemish on the face of our carefully manicured ornamental gardens and monotonous green lawns. In reality, the term *weed* simply refers to any unwanted plant, and for us as modern charmers, our wants are perhaps a little different than those of the upper-class garden society. Horsetail, dock, ragweed, shepherd's purse, bull nettle, pokeweed, and fleabane would all be considered "weeds" by one who does not want them, but they are also all useful in different ways for our craft. When we release the urge to manicure the land around us and restrict its growth based on our own desires, when we allow a meadow to simply be a meadow, we are able to meet ancient beings who have been waiting for us all along. If you are lucky enough to have some land or a yard of your own, consider allowing a patch to grow of its own accord, and watch what happens. The first year will largely be tall grass, since grass has probably been dropping its seeds there for a very long time. Eventually, though, your meadow patch will, of its own accord, erupt in diversity, and the plants that grow there will be a better representation of the wild flora around you, drawing birds and other creatures who rely on these plants to survive.

Much of the work of walking and meeting plants is done in the summer, but in the fall and winter, there is also work that can be done. The plant's body reaches both above and below the soil line, straddling two worlds. Digging up the roots of a plant we know can often lead to surprising discoveries that can be used later on to discern more about its nature. The root of the common dandelion, for instance, is surprisingly substantial, revealing the interesting dichotomy that is essential to its nature, being both a solar and a saturnine plant, a creature of bright exuberance in the spring months who also reaches deep below us, into the underworld or chthonic realms. How amazing it is to think that this "common weed" is possessed of both vital and chthonic energies, announcing itself as a spirit connected to both the living and the dead. Aside from gathering roots, we can also use the colder months to gather dried twigs, which can be tied with twine into various ephemera to call the spirit into the home, such as the equal-armed rowan crosses popular in Scottish folk magic. Dried stalks may be soaked in water in order to soften them, then braided into ornamental "dollies," a fitting vessel for the plant spirit and a charm to bring luck to one's home. Branches may yield the material necessary for a witch's stang or staff. Ripe seeds from dried flowers and fruits can be placed in a dedicated vessel, a way of housing the spirit until the coming of spring. Dried berries can be gathered, and if still soft, strung on thread. (We should, of course, be especially careful of possible toxicity when dealing with berries and fruits.) I'm fond of speaking to the plant while I gather seeds, telling her that I'm glad she had a good year on my land, and that I'm collecting these seeds so that she may return again.

Even in these early stages of meeting green spirits, it is not uncommon to receive signals that the plant spirit recognizes you and is eager to interact with you. This is more likely if you are able to make some form of regular offering, such as a drink of water poured at the plant's base or simply kind words of welcome and encouragement. Watch carefully for the sudden breeze that causes flowers to nod. Listen for the sounds of birds and insects trilling around you while you speak to the plant. Most importantly, be aware of how you feel while in the plant's presence. You might even consider, at these early stages, asking the plant's permission to take a portion of its earthly body so that it may be dried and preserved indoors. Tie the plant into a bundle, and hang it to dry, or press a leaf or flower between the pages of a journal. Interact with it regularly, and be mindful of your dreams, for they may offer signals of connection with the spirit. The mind is more connected to the otherworld than we know, and the thing we call our consciousness is, I believe, intertwined with the spiritual ecosystems around us in a way that is inseparable and interdependent.

I do recognize that not everyone has access to green space around them. If it is necessary to purchase dried plant matter or a prepared herbal product, we can still take the time to make initial contact with the spirit. Consider transferring the dried herb, tincture, essence, or what have you to a new vessel bought or fashioned especially for this purpose. Take a moment to thank the plant for its difficult journey, and explain your reason for purchasing it. Speak some of its old folk names. Find a likeness of the plant in its mature, growing form, and hold it in your mind as you offer a gentle welcome. Use the simple ritual of hallowing the leaves, if you wish, but by whatever means you prefer to use, treat the plant you have bought not as a "thing," but as an embodied aspect of an ancient spirit, regardless of how it came to you. This is a good way to begin repairing the indignity and desecration that has likely been a part of its journey.

Witchcraft is, at its core, a form of animist spirituality, recognizing the living spirit within all things human and otherwise.

While most of us are taught from an early age to pray to a god of some form or other, interacting with the spirits of flora and fauna is different, for they do not claim to be our creators or our lord, and they do not demand our worship. What they do want from us is as complicated and varied as the wants of any community of living beings. We are not seeking a master to serve or a djinn to subjugate to our will, but instead, a neighbor, friend, and ally in our craft. The way in which we interact with a spirit that is neither our master nor our servant is much the same way we might interact with a neighbor: reciprocity. Even spirits have wants and desires, and we can offer things in exchange for the spirit's aid in our witchcraft. Over time, and with patience, these relationships can become less transactional and more loving.

This shift towards an animist consciousness can and should affect how we interact with living beings in our daily life. How long has it been, do you think, since someone thanked the dandelion spirit where you live for its joyful, yellow blooms? More likely, humans have sprayed it with poison, uprooted it without purpose, or cursed it for making its home in their flowerbeds. It could be that it has been a very long time indeed since the dandelion spirit where you live has witnessed kindness from a witch. As human beings, we are often mistaken as outsiders by the spirits of flora and fauna, for humans have a long history of wreaking havoc upon the natural world, killing not for survival, but for pleasure. As witches, though, we have a certain spiritual harmony with these beings, especially the unwanted "weeds," and if we act with patience and kindness, spirits will slowly begin to recognize us as their kin.

The Language of Growing Things

When we pay close attention to the appearance and behavior of plants, we notice that they are not mute, inanimate things at all, but are constantly transforming and expressing themselves. Some produce thorns to ward off animals. Others erupt with sweet-scented blooms to attract pollinators. The living things that we call plants are actually quite diverse and varied in the ways they behave in the world. These keys, along with our own spiritual perception of plant spirits and the folklore surrounding them, can be used in order to identify the plant's magical signatures.

While I understand the temptation to refer to a magical catalogue of plant correspondences, I do strongly recommend forming your own understanding of the plant spirit's properties. "Reading" the language of the plant spirit for oneself is such an enjoyable part of building one's own craft. It is empowering for the witch and plant alike, leading to a stronger bond, and often resulting in surprising discoveries that are not catalogued in books already. Consider that the folklore of plants comes to us from an actual place, an actual time, and an actual culture of people who once interacted with the plant regularly. I consider learning the folklore of the plant and the reading of its magical signatures to be equally important and interdependent, one alone meaning little without the other. When we divorce the folkloric knowledge of the plant from the first-hand experience of its presence, we are left something lesser than the whole, disconnected from the wisdom that was the key to its potency in the first place. All magical knowledge of plants comes from a community or individual who once interacted with the plant and its spirit, and if we are to tap into the root of this craft, we must do the same and experience it for ourselves. This is merely another expression of an old principle in witchcraft that rings true across many aspects of practice: if we wish to become as mighty as the charmers of old, we, like them, *must drink from the source*, building our craft the way they built it and experiencing what they themselves would have experienced. Second-hand knowledge is like a map in some ways. Is a map helpful when plotting our course? Absolutely. Is looking at a map a substitute for experiencing the place itself? No, it is not.

The first and most obvious step is to begin understanding the plant spirit through the appearance and behavior of its earthly body. What does the plant look like? How does it grow? And how might we group plants based on these perceived attributes? A bit of magical history can help with this. In the 17th century, herbalist

Nicholas Culpeper described certain conditions that grouped plants under astrological influences. These largely related to the plant's supposed effects on a certain part of the human body that was ruled by a sign in the heavens or a planetary body, among other things. But Culpeper was hardly alone in his approach; other astrological botanists, often with a more mystical or occult interest, grouped plants by a variety of such "signatures." In his 16th century work *Phytognomonica*, Giambattista della Porta described the astrological rulership of plants as relating to shape and form. Thus, leaves, flowers, and pods that bear a lunar shape would identify a plant as being ruled, at least in part, by the Moon. In the same century, Paracelsus, otherwise known as Theophrastus von Hohenheim, asserted that each plant was the terrestrial form of a particular star, and each star the heavenly form of a grouping of plants.

While all of this may seem very heady stuff, it has, over the years, found its way into folk methods of magical herbalism via the slow circulation of old knowledge that persisted in rural areas. Even today, there are farmers who plant and gather by the moon and the signs of the stars. Though Porta and Paracelsus' systems may seem ornate, they are, at their core, simply another expression of the old folk-magical principle of *sympathy* (sometimes called *simulacra*), which suggests, at its most basic level, that two things bearing similarity share a magical connection. This is the principle behind the infamous witches' poppet, the use of sigils and seals to represent desired outcomes, and even the selection of color when choosing a candle for a working. "Like affects like," as the old adage says. The other key folk-magical principle, known as *contagion*, will come into play later in both the creation and usage of herbal preparations.

We can expand upon the systems of the old occult herbalists by examining the plant closely as a spiritual and physical being with its own potencies, properties, and hallmarks. Bear in mind that these are tendencies and patterns, not hard and fast rules. There are many exceptions, as we will find in the individual entries on herbal folklore in the latter section of this book. Still, painting with a very wide brush, we can identify some characteristics that relate to planetary influence and at least help us describe in general terms the personality of the plant before us.

Solar plants (those ruled by the Sun) often bear round flowers that resemble the Sun in their appearance. Their flowers are often yellow, but not always. This includes many members of the aster family, such as daisies and sunflowers. They tend to thrive in full sunlight, sometimes with flowers or leaves that open with the sun and close at night. Many solar plants bear blooms that face the sun directly. The properties of these plants tend to echo the solar qualities of health, wholeness, joy, and fulfillment. They are often used in very general blessings, but also in the restoration of health and wellness.

Lunar plants (those ruled by the Moon) tend bear crescent shapes or drooped, hanging shapes in their forms. Think of the droop-necked snowdrop flower or the crescent-shaped seed pod of the wisteria. They may also contain a great deal of water within their bodies, and often bear pale blooms or a pale color to their leaves and stalks. Lunar plants may bear flowers that open at night and often prefer cooler temperatures. These plants are often used in divination, dream-work, and charms to do with either madness or stillness of mind. One can think of lunar potencies as being a mirror of the Sun; while solar magics create a joy that is wholesome and embodied, lunar magics bring an ecstasy that is exciting and disembodied.

Martial plants (those ruled by Mars) may have leaves or flowers in the shape of weapons, such as spears, knives, or arrows. They also tend to bear thorns, cause pain or rashes upon touching them, or bear other hallmarks of strong defense systems against those who would harm them. These plants are often used in protection charms, warding, and curse-work, though of a less malefic variety than one might achieve with saturnine plants. They are also used to achieve victory in all manner of conflict and challenge. We can think of martial potency as a rugged, strong, vibrant warrior or athlete, eager to rise to the challenge and dominate opponents. While we sometimes associate these qualities with masculinity, it is more helpful to think of martial powers as defined by vitality and zest for life. Regardless of our gender, the desire to protect our loved ones and leave our mark on the world is basic and human and quite healthy when held in balance.

Mercurial plants (those ruled by Mercury) tend to have hairy bodies or very fine leaves, such that they are easily blown and jostled. These plants may bear shapes that resemble wings or feathers. They may release seeds that are tufted or ride upon the breeze in order to distribute themselves. They may also release an odor that is not sweet, but also not unpleasant, such as sage or dill. Mercurial powers are tricky to define. The mundane or non-magical meaning of the word *mercurial* refers to a nature that is rapidly shifting, tempestuous, and subject to change. Mercury, as we will see when examining the planetary hexagram, is of a mingled nature by its very definition. Generally, though, mercurial herbs have been used to aid in communication, exchanges, travel, business deals, and any activity involving movement and transformation.

Jovial plants (those ruled by Jupiter) tend to tower over other plants, becoming quite tall in stature. They appear to be reaching for the heavens. They may be prolific in their dispersion of seeds and fruits, covering an area or scattering widely in order to generate as many new plants as possible. These plants are often associated with fertility, prosperity, success in legal matters, and the achievement of power and authority. They are also sometimes associated with simple luck charms. Jovial potency achieves dominion in a way very different from martial potency; it seeks social power, often in the form of the respect of one's colleagues and community or election or promotion to positions of authority. Think of the dominating nature of jovial plants as a king on a throne, strategizing to maintain power through secret plots and alliances. This differs markedly from the style of domination employed by Mars, which is more like a raging warrior on a battlefield. Jovial potency values order, peace, and prosperity for all, which also differentiates it from saturnine magics, which seek to subvert or disrupt order by opening gates between worlds.

Venereal plants (those ruled by Venus) may have blooms or leaves that bear a striking resemblance to genitalia, breasts, or buttocks (which includes the heart shape). They tend to release a sweet, enticing fragrance and bear large, attractive flowers. Such plants sometimes attract more pollinators than others, being covered in the warm months with bees, moths, and butterflies. We usually think of venereal magics as having to do with charms for love, beauty, popularity, friendship, and desire, but there is more to them than this. Just as martial potency sometimes seeks to dominate others through aggression, venereal potency sometimes seeks to subdue others through charm and guile, to penetrate an enemy's defenses with a smile or carefully placed word. In its more wholesome aspects, venereal herbs can be used to strengthen the bonds of love: both toward others and inward, toward oneself. This latter form need not necessarily devolve into narcissism; seeing oneself as worthy of love and kindness is often the first step towards recovery for those who have lived through trauma.

Saturnine plants (those ruled by Saturn) tend to grow a substantial underground root system, often with a large taproot, reaching deep into the underworld. These plants may also bear poisonous qualities, like some of the nightshades, or prefer growing in "waste places," such as trenches, roadsides, and disturbed earth. Unlike martial herbs, these plants tend not to wear their defenses on the outside. They can be beautiful and alluring, their outwardly charm belying their inner poisons. These plants often appear in the old witch-lore, and it is worth noting that witches have much in common with these plants, witches themselves being possessed of a hidden nature that is not visible on the outside. It is also worth noting that a poisonous plant is not, in and of itself, wicked or evil. All living things simply want to thrive, and after all, we are only poisoned if we touch or ingest it, a choice made by the human being and not the plant itself. Saturnine plants are often used magically for spirit work, necromancy, and the arts of cursing. They are also used in achieving spirit flight and sabbatic ekstasis, a state of consciousness in which we step outside of the physical body and experience the spiritual communion that is sometimes called "the witch's sabbat." Unlike the potency of Jupiter, which values order and stability, the potency of Saturn is a disrupter and trickster, seeking to open unexpected gates to the otherworld, like the old folktales in which a protagonist accidentally stumbles into elphame or fairyland. Needless to say, it is possible to poison oneself when working with many of these plants, so I must here recommend working with them using the safe alternative formulas provided in the recipe section.

These categories are not exclusive, meaning that a plant can be both saturnine and mercurial at once in different aspects. A single plant could, feasibly, bear hallmarks of as many as five planetary rulers—though it is likely that some planetary influences are more dominant than others. Even so, these guidelines are still somewhat limited for understanding a plant's full personality. We can expand upon this yet further in order to analyze the plant more carefully for its magical properties, however complex they may be.

Bear in mind that the goal here is not to overwhelm ourselves by creating an exhaustive listing of the plant's characteristics. Our analysis need not go on to the point of tedium. Rather, we are really hoping to capture what stands out about this plant, what makes it unique among its neighbors, and what qualities we notice first when we encounter it. Consider using the questions below to help you pluck out the most dominant keys in the plant's appearance and behavior. These will unlock part of its personality and open the way to working with the plant more deeply. Don't worry about making your way through every single question for every plant you meet; instead, use these questions to guide your analysis of the most prominent, expressive, and unique qualities you notice right away.

Here, then, are some key questions to guide a more in-depth magical analysis of the plant's body and the meanings hidden therein:

In what season does the plant mature? When does it die or slumber? *Our seasons carry meanings that are often associated with the agricultural cycle and the ancient festivals of our premodern ancestors. Spring is a time of renewal and beginnings. Summer is a time of work and collaboration. Fall is a time of harvest, celebration, and increasing darkness. Winter is a time of rest and* withdrawal for most plants, with the exception of evergreens and a few others.

Does the plant grow humbly and low to the ground, or does it tower over its neighbors? *Plants that grow tall and mighty, especially over a short growth cycle, may be found to have an aggressive nature and a dominating influence.*

What distinct colors do you notice on its blooms and leaves? *In Scottish folklore, red suggests the vitality of blood. Yellow, in the language of flowers, often signifies joy. Color associations vary wildly, but should be kept in mind in the context of your own culture and background. What does the color of the plant announce to you?*

How substantial is the plant's root system? Is it an annual or perennial? *Plants that are annual, living and dying in the course of a single year, may have a less chthonic or underworldly nature than those that establish a long-lived root system under the soil. Plants with a deep taproot reaching into the realms of the dead are sometimes described as having a saturnine (Saturn-related) quality.*

What scent does the plant release, and how does it make you feel? *Mints tend to have a very strong aromatic quality which is sometimes described as a "clean" smell, but not always. Dead nettles, for instance, have a mustier scent that is more complex. Roses and other sweet-smelling flowers are often described as having a venereal (Venus-related) nature, being attuned to feeling and matters of the heart, but also to beauty and vanity. Do use caution here; not all plants are safe to smell up close.*

Do the leaves and flowers point up toward the sun or downward toward the soil? *Plants that express an upright posture often embody more extroverted and open natures, whereas plants with a drooped posture can sometimes be more secretive and reluctant to reveal their wisdom to those deemed unworthy. A sloped curve on a flower that droops can sometimes indicate a lunar potency, mirroring the shape of a crescent.*

Do the flowers close at night, opening for the sun? *Blooms that open to face the sunlight may indicate a strong solar nature at work within a plant.*

Do the flowers close during the day, opening for the moon? *Similarly to the previous point, these plants may embody a more lunar or nocturnal nature.*

Does the plant prefer to grow in full sun or shade? *Herbs that flourish in shady areas may have more quiet, gentle, or introverted natures than those that can withstand a great deal of sunlight.*

Is the material of the plant thin and light, or is it thick and full of water? *Watery plants can signal a lunar nature, but more importantly, these plants often embody a potency of retention, the ability to hold and keep their energy within themselves.*

Do the flowers resemble anything (faces, animals, skulls, etc.)? *Many plants are named after these resemblances, and such likenesses are ingrained in their magical folklore. Skullcap, for instance, is named for its resemblance to headwear in previous ages. Dandelion comes from the French "dent de lion," its jagged leaves resembling the teeth of a lion.*

Do the leaves resemble anything (hearts, spears, etc.)? *The heart-shaped leaves of the violet have been long associated with matters of love, while the spear-shaped leaves of mugwort are often associated with protection.*

Is the plant safe to touch? If so, is the plant soft and pleasant to touch, or is it thorny or irritating? *The presence of many thorns or harmful oils on a plant (such as poison ivy or poison oak) often signifies a relationship with Mars and a nature that is combative, aggressive, and well-suited to protection and even cursing. Conversely, a plant that is covered in soft, downy hairs and is pleasant to the touch may have a gentle, comforting nature.*

Are the leaves and flowers singular in nature, or do they contain multiple, complex, thinner or smaller flowers or leaves? *Plants that stretch themselves into many units with much air passing between their parts can sometimes be possessed of a mercurial nature. These spirits may have powers of communication, exchange, and intellect.*

Does the plant release a great many seeds at once, or only a few? *Plants that are prolific, aggressively distributing many seeds at once may have a nature related to Jupiter. These plant spirits tend to have a fertile, domineering quality that sometimes lends itself to energies of success and ambition.*

Does the plant prefer disturbed soil and "waste places" (roadsides, construction sites, recent digging, trenches and channels, etc.)? *Plants that thrive in these places may also be saturnine in a different way, for they often emit an "outsider" energy, sowing their seeds away from the masses of other plants.*

Does the plant prefer sandy, dry soil with little water? *This may indicate a plant with strong reserves of energy, capable of enduring many challenges and outlasting others.*

What sorts of insects and birds are drawn to the plant? *Plants that emit a foul, rotting smell, for instance, tend to attract flies, associating the plant's nature with decay and decomposition, which is to say the release of that which cannot be held onto any longer. A plant that attracts bees may have a sweet nature or even a matriarchal quality to it.*

Another important part of understanding a plant's nature is its history of use. This history matters because it has defined much of the plant's relationship with humans through the ages, and this repeated pattern of activity has shaped how the plant spirit will approach us and interact with us. We can hardly discern the magical properties of elder, for instance, without at least being aware of its long history of use against the common cold. For the work of researching a plant's history of use, I heartily recommend two key sources: Culpeper's *Complete Herbal* (also called *The English Physician*) and Grieve's *A Modern Herbal*. Both of these works are encyclopedic in nature and available online. Culpeper's work, being from the 1600s, provides a more historical understanding of the plant's uses hundreds of years ago. (It's also full of amusing asides and antiquated plant names, such as *piss-a-bed*, an old folk name for dandelion.) Grieve's work is legendary and provides both historical and relatively modern plant uses. Keep in mind that we aren't following their recommendations for crafting medicines; our purposes are magical, not medical, and our preparations from these plants will be quite different from the ones they recommend.

Lastly, but most importantly, we must always take time to contemplate the folklore of the plant. The latter section of this book is full of examples that might help you in contemplating the folkloric threads behind various plants you may encounter. While we can discern much from the visible signatures in the body of the plant and its history of use in human hands, folklore matters greatly, for it is how the plant spirit crosses into the discourse of dreams and visions, how its matter gives way to an undying form preserved in our storytelling and our wish-making. If folklore is a kind of shared dream, arising over generations, then the lore of the plant is the distillation of who the plant spirit is, and has been, to generations of charmers who came before us.

In many cases, the lore of a plant is preserved in its name and in the etymological origins of words. The burdock, for example, derives part of its name from the Latin *burra*, meaning a piece of wool. This is because sheep's wool would often be found clinging to the barbed heads of burdock plants in pastures. The humble dandelion's name comes from the French *dent-de-lion*, meaning "lion's tooth." This is due to the toothed shape of its leaves. The mullein was, at one time, called *hag's taper*, and it was believed that witches used the long stalks of mullein plants as candles in secret rites. There is a related bit of history here in the historic use of mullein among ancient Roman funerary practices, but feel free to read that under Mullein's entry in the third section. The point is that these names reveal the ways older generations interacted with the plant and what characteristics in them they found most distinct, contributing to the lore of the plant over many generations. Names preserve a kind of fingerprint, a unique understanding of the plant's personality, and names should be considered carefully when discerning magical potencies at work in the plant's nature.

When searching for the lore of a particular plant, do check the latter section of this book, but do also consider consulting one or more of the following works, which are trusted guides to the plant lore of previous ages:

Thistleton-Dyer, T. F. (1889). *The Folk-Lore of Plants.*

Thistleton-Dyer's work is incredibly ripe with references to superstitions, stories, and customs related to a great variety of plants. While the book weaves together the stories of different plants beautifully, this does make it difficult to consult as a reference work. Thankfully, there are several online versions available for free (via gutenberg.org and similar archives), and these are largely searchable, a useful strategy when hunting down lore on a particular herb.

Folkard. R. (1884). *Plant Lore, Legends, and Lyrics: Embracing the Myths, Superstitions, Traditions, and Folk-Lore of the Plant Kingdom.*

Like Thistleton-Dyer's work, *Plant Lore*'s first section organizes the lore of plants around themes, including plants associated with witches, faeries, and the Devil. Folkard's second section, however, is imminently practical, being an alphabetical listing of plants and their surrounding tales and superstitions. I do still recommend searching the online version of this work, though, since not all of Folkard's notes from the first section are duplicated in the encyclopedic section of the book.

Northcote, R. (1903). *The Book of Herbs.*

Northcote's work is peppered with literary references to herbs and flowers that are lovely and amusing, if not always helpful for the magical herbalist. While most of the author's notes concern history of use, there is a substantial amount of superstition and folklore included here, so it is worth at least searching the online version of this charming text when learning the folklore of a plant that is new to you.

Waterman, C. H. (1839). *Flora's Lexicon: An Interpretation of the Language and Sentiment of Flowers.*

Waterman's work is devoted to the Victorian language of flowers, meaning the ways sentiments (both kind-hearted and less than kind) were expressed using floral arrangements. The book's scope is quite impressive, but I do recommend using this work as a starting point for flower lore. Many of the Victorian floral associations have quite ancient roots that one does not come across unless consulting other volumes. *Flora's Lexicon* is, like the others, available in an online version that is searchable.

Deas, L. (1898). *Flower Favourites: Their Legends, Symbolism, and Significance.*

Deas work is organized around the lore and myths of individual flowers beloved for their ornamental beauty, and though not exactly extensive, the depth of lore included on each entry is very rich, including references to legends from many parts of the world and across many ages. *Flower Favourites* is also available online for free.

In addition, one might consider consulting others works listed in the bibliography at the end of this book, for many of these volumes are available via libraries or the internet free of charge, and one can often stumble across a bit of lore this way in order to verify popular sayings or folk wisdom from our own upbringing.

As you discover the patterns, behaviors, histories, and other magical keys of the plants around you, be sure to record them in your personal grimoire. This will allow you to refer back to their properties with ease later, which you will appreciate when preparing formulas from plants.

Conjuring the Green Spirit

In order to begin working with plant spirits in our magic, we must first be able to perceive them. This is one of many points of irony in the craft: that the art of conjuring spirits is not truly about compelling them to appear, but about permitting ourselves to perceive them. It is ourselves we conjure—the part of us that is able and willing to make the otherworldly encounter. We are opening a door and inviting the other to join us for a time, but in order to converse with them, we must be present with them in that space between worlds.

Obviously, we should not expect physical manifestations, temperature changes, objects flying off shelves, or any other silly Hollywood tropes. Our expectations of spirit work must be in line with reality. We will likely perceive images, sensations, sounds, words, flavors, or even scents in our mind's eye. We might simply have "feelings," which can communicate a great deal when interpreted carefully. In the absence of these, we can also interpret the movement of smoke, the flicker of the candle, or divinations via sortilege—such as tarot, ogham, or runes—to receive communication from the spirit. Set these as your expectations, and you will not be disappointed. If, in the process of this work, you perceive the spirit as physically present or find yourself unable to distinguish visions from reality, do stop and seek counseling, as this is the definition of a hallucination. This is not a recommendation in jest. Much of witchcraft is about self-knowledge and self-control, and the mind must be healthy and sharp if we are to be successful. The images and impressions we sometimes receive through witch-sight are spiritual, not physical, and though these impressions can be very strong at times, the distinction should always be very clear, resulting in no confusion.

In order to achieve what is called *witch-sight* or simply *the sight*, it is helpful to employ the arts of *ekstasis*, which is to say, ritual practices aimed at stepping outside of ordinary consciousness. In essence, we are stepping, for a moment, outside of the self in order to experience what lies beyond it. These practices are ancient and appear in virtually every culture on earth. In witchcraft, these visionary experiences are related to what we call "spirit flight," which is, in fact, the origin of the folkloric trope of the flying witch. Our goal, however, is not fully transvective, for we do not need to leave the space of the physical body; our goal is to loosen the spirit just enough to perceive the otherworld around us.

For those who are new to the practice of awakening the sight, I can recommend a good starting exercise:

To Awaken the Sight

Begin simply, sitting upon the floor or at a table in a comfortable chair. The room should be quite dark except for a single lit candle placed before you. Darkness is an ally here, for it allows the hidden parts of the mind to come out to play and loosens the stranglehold of empirical, rational thought.

Once you are comfortable, begin moving your hands before and behind the candle, playing with the shadow forms made by the interruption of the candle's light, breathing in time with these movements.

Next, close your eyes, and use your hands to create shadows that pass over your closed eyelids. Notice the levels of darkness here: the dark of the room with the candle, the dark of closing your eyes, and the dark of the shadow passing over the eyelid. Many creatures are quite sensitive to light, and the gentle dark signals to them that they are safe, that they are able to emerge now from their hiding place, free from the eyes of predators. Consider that, in some ways, witches are among these creatures. Most of the time, we must wear a kind of costume in order to function in the world, driving to work, tending to children, completing chores and tasks that only pile up time and time again. In this space, allow yourself to remove that costume.

Permit the ripples of the shadows passing over your eyelids to become waves washing away your mundane self. That old costume will still be there, of course, waiting for you. But for now, let it go. You may feel the urge to sway or contort your body almost as if stretching awake from a long sleep. You may even experience a slight euphoria as you do so. This is perfectly normal. At the very least, you should feel deeply relaxed and at peace, almost as if setting down a weight you did not know you were carrying or removing a thick coat that you did not know you were wearing. Remember this feeling, for it is, I think, a lesson. Witchcraft, at its core, is not about performing ornate charms or conjuring mighty spirits; it is the removal of invisible restraints that have caused us to forget the mythic, ancient, ensouled beings that we already are. All of our other charms and conjurations stem from this truth, and much of our art is aimed at resisting and loosening those restraints in a variety of ways.

Once the feeling of release has been achieved, we have entered a state of *ekstasis*. It is now that we should begin turning our awareness to the space around us. You might open your eyes, or you might leave them closed. It matters not. You will most likely perceive a world around you that is somehow more permeable and less fixed than it was before. Images and impressions may enter your mind in a way that feels dream-like. If you sense something dangerous or frightening, remember that you can always stop. Slapping your hands upon the floor, your thighs, or a table (being mindful of the candle), will shift your awareness back quite quickly to the mundane world.

Once you are able to use your witch-sight with some degree of control, you may wish to move on to a new exercise and attempt to perceive the plant spirit. This will allow us to make a more direct form of spirit contact than we were able to make before. In this practice, we are reaching out to the spirit directly with a gentle greeting, a simple skill that will be endlessly useful in daily life when interacting with the plants around us. Though it is not required, it is helpful to have some old words—a song of sorts—to call the spirit of the plant out of its resting place and into our presence. While many witches prefer to write their own calls to the spirit, I do find a pleasure in drawing from old words that have been used over generations. The benefit of this is also practical in nature; the plant spirit has likely heard some version of this invitation before, and they may be more likely to recognize us as members of a greater tradition that has perhaps included human allies in the past. This is much like introducing yourself to a stranger by mentioning a parent or relative they may already know.

There are a few hallmarks of verbal spirit conjurations that we can rely on when crafting our own call. One option comes to us from the *Lacnunga*, a tenth century Anglo-Saxon book of charms:

Remember, thou Mugwort, what thou hast revealed,
What thou hast sworn at the great proclamation:
Thou art strong against three and against thirty.
Thou art strong against poisons and flying poisons.
Thou art strong against the foe who wanders through the land.

At the center of this charm is the invocation of an ancient pact made even before the sorcerer's birth. Consider that many plants have a history of use dating back hundreds or even thousands of years. Consider that when we engage with these plants spiritually, we are acting as the latest in a long line of witches forging relationships with these ancient beings. This language reflects that legacy, and can be adapted to work with other plants, relying on phrasings like "remember, thou [name of herb], what thou hast revealed" and "thou art strong against/for [magical purpose]."

Yet another may be derived from the *Grimorium Verum*, a grimoire of magic from the 1700s:

Osurmy ✠ *Delmusan* ✠ *Atalsloym* ✠ *Charusihoa* ✠ *Melany Liamintho* ✠ *Colehon* ✠ *Paron* ✠ *Madoin* ✠ *Merloy* ✠ *Bulerator* ✠ *Donmeo* ✠ *Hone* ✠ *Peloym* ✠ *Ibasil* ✠ *Meon Alymdrictels* ✠ *Person* ✠ *Crisolsay* ✠ *Lemon Selse Nidar* ✠ *Horiel Peunt* ✠ *Halmon* ✠ *Asophiel* ✠ *Ilnostreon* ✠ *Baniel* ✠ *Vermias* ✠ *Eslevor* ✠ *Noelma* ✠ *Dorsamot* ✠ *Lhavala* ✠ *Omot* ✠ *Frangam* ✠ *Beldor* ✠ *Dragin* ✠ *I conjure thee, spirit of [—]* ✠

A particularly lovely spoken herbal charm for harvesting comes from the *Carmina Gadelica*, a collection of Scottish incantations that is very close to my heart:

> *I will cull the gracious root*
> *As Brigit culled it with her one hand,*
> *To put essence in breast and gland of milk,*
> *To put substance in udder and in kidney.*

Note that the lines beginning with "to put" begins the listing of the uses of the plant in this charm, a pattern we may adapt in order to suit the particular plant we are working with.

I am sometimes fond of using my own adaptation of a spoken charm that is quite old. One earlier version of the "Haile Be" charm appears in Reginald Scot's 1500s text, *The Discoverie of Witchcraft*, but my own version is as follows:

> *Hail be, thou holy herb,*
> *Plucked from the ground,*
> *Friend unto the people,*
> *In love and kinship bound.*
> *Thou hast healed many a wound*
> *And soothed many a pain.*
> *Awaken now to keep thy word*
> *In our Lady's name.*

Alternatively, when working with dark or baneful herbs, or simply those aligned with saturnine or martial properties, I sometimes use a variation on this charm:

> *Hail be, thou holy herb,*
> *Plucked from the ground,*
> *Friend unto the poisoner,*
> *In wrath and vengeance bound.*
> *Thou hast ruined many a lord*
> *And wounded many a king.*
> *Awaken now to keep thy word*
> *In the Devil's name.*

(Do note that the language here is intentionally venomous in order to awaken the dark properties of the plant; our goal is never to actually poison a human being.)

Choose any of these methods, or choose none at all and fashion your own call from scratch. What matters is that we take a moment to call to the spirit of the plant, to awaken it from its dormant state of rest. Sometimes, when calling to a plant spirit, I prefer simply to hum a familiar folk tune, one the plant may have heard some version of a very long time ago, signaling to them that I know them, and that it is safe to know me. Record one or more of your preferred methods of calling to the spirit in your personal grimoire.

But there is one more piece that that must be added to the ritual we are about to attempt: access to the currency of the otherworld, which is to say, spiritual nourishment. This nourishment is the dark bread beneath our very feet. Elphame, the otherworldly realm of witch-kin, the dead, and the fae, was in olden times said to lie deep beneath the earth. Sometimes, the lore is more specific, identifying the hidden realm as lying just outside of the boundary of hell. This was perhaps a way of reconciling the surviving pagan beliefs of the faery faith with the more binary Christian cosmology that defined all things as "good" or "bad," "holy" or "unholy." For ancient peoples, who were both pagan and animist in their belief systems, the unseen dark beneath us was quite literally *where the dead went*. Their bodies returned to the land, and their spirits were there as well. Not only their spirits, mind you, but all living things that came before, flora and fauna all, returning and mingling in the source of all nourishment, the hidden place from which emerges the seed that would become grain to nourish the people. The realm of the dead is, in this simpler cosmology, also the realm that gives all life. The otherworld, be it called Elphame or by any other term, is in some ways a poetic rendering of a certain deeper truth: *all life begins and ends in the land beneath us.*

We can draw on this currency by magical means, and though the process is deceptively simple, it is a powerful way to form a bond with a plant spirit (and indeed many other kinds of spirits), for we are speaking for a moment in their language rather than our own. This technique builds upon the breath portion of the ritual of hallowing the leaves, but the breath here must be rooted in power in order to be received as a true offering, which is of course our intention. We must "pull in" the dark nourishment of the otherworld beneath our feet as we inhale, and allow that nourishment to pass through us on the exhale. This is similar to the ways trees will use their roots to share nourishment, sometimes across great distances. Practice this breathing exercise on your own at first. With your witch sight, *feel out* the sea of dark soil beneath you, and as you inhale slowly, pull it up from the soles of your feet. It should feel slightly cold, heavy, and quieting—like the air of an old cellar with a dirt floor, or like the chill air of the morning after a hard rain has disturbed the soil. Let it fill you from the bottom up, then let it pour out and through you as you exhale. Practice this technique until you feel confident.

To attempt to call to the spirit, we should be in proximity to the plant itself, though this can take many forms. On a biochemical level, plants respond to the vibrations of sound quite readily; on a spiritual level, even more so. If the plant is dangerous to you for any reason, we can begin simply sitting or standing next to the living plant in its environment. There is no need to damage, uproot, or even touch the plant for this work if it isn't safe for you to do so. This method may also be preferable if the plant is rare or endangered, or if we simply haven't worked much with the plant before, as it is more respectful—at least in the early stages. Although somewhat similar to hallowing the leaves, this ritual is different, for it involves a more thorough incantation and entails an offering to the spirit to entice it to closer communion with the practitioner, which will later prove useful when we attempt to perform herbal charms of all kinds. All herbal charms, using the process I will provide in this book, build on the practice of calling in the spirit, so I encourage you to take your time with this step until it "feels" right to you and you are confident in your abilities.

To Call to the Plant Spirit

To call to the plant spirit, we must of course be near its living or preserved body. Connecting with a live plant in this way is helpful for accessing the plant's vital current. If it is not possible to work with the living plant, we can certainly begin with a portion of its dried leaves, roots, or flowers. These can be simply placed in a bowl (choose something beautiful) and set before us on a table or counter surface. This process can actually stimulate the potency of old herbs that have been dried and sealed away for a very long time or plant matter that has been purchased online. Just be sure that whatever you have bought has been transferred to a new container, preferably glass or ceramic—something with more dignity than a plastic bag.

To begin, recall the feeling of the ecstatic state you achieved earlier. This may feel strange since you may be outdoors, surrounded by more light and noise and activity than when you performed this exercise alone, but I'll let you in on a secret: *you are the same being everywhere you go.* The state of mind we experience in a closed ritual space is accessible to us anywhere at all. In a public place, it is unlikely that we will achieve the euphoric state accessible to us in private, but that is no matter, for all we really need is a gentle shift—a slight and subtle budge out of our mundane consciousness and into the otherworld. The key, I often find, is to remember the feeling vividly. Relive, in your mind's eye, the feeling you achieved before, and allow that "self" you were able to shed before to loosen just a bit. A slight budge is all that is needed.

With your witch-sight at work, and with your hands raised near the plant itself—not touching, but close, as if you were gently cupping them around a very large butterfly or moth—enunciate the call. Speak the words or hum the tune of your chosen incantation softly and slowly. We are not medieval mages shouting at some poor, abused spirit caged within a vessel; we are merely witches calling to a green friend. Usually, a voice barely above a whisper will do the trick nicely. As before, watch for signs in the wind, the nodding of flowers, or the sounds of birds, crickets, or other wildlife. If you are indoors working with a purchased herb, consider lighting a simple candle nearby so that the spirit can offer a simple gesture through the flicker and wave of its flame. Even if you do not receive images or impressions with your witch-sight, there should be some sign that your call has been received and answered, which can often arrive as a simple "feeling" or inexplicable "knowing."

When you are able to sense the presence of the plant spirit, make the offering of the breath. Remember that this breath must be drawn from below, full and potent, in order to be received as an offering. If it is received kindly, we may sense reciprocation in the form of a change in the air around us. Plant spirits (and most spirits, really) respect the principle of reciprocity more thoroughly than human beings. You may feel lighter or more energized after offering the breath. You may even sense the plant spirit "smiling," which is a strange feeling that is difficult to describe, but unmistakable when it occurs. If working with dried and preserved plant matter, the spirit may not be able to reciprocate in this way, but you will likely sense a change in the feel of the plant's body, a quickening even stronger than you did when performing the hallowing of the leaves. In this case, the reciprocation is in the gifting of a portion of its ensouled body to us, for our magical use.

Though it appears simple, I find this ritual of calling to the plant spirit to be incredibly versatile and powerful. By calling to the spirit, we are stimulating and quickening its potencies on a subtle level already, even without working a specific charm or crafting an herbal preparation. In this moment, the plant spirit is touching us, and we are touching it. Some of our spirit has rubbed off on the plant, and some of its spirit has been temporarily imbued upon us. We should not be surprised, then, if the effect of the ritual lingers for a bit, causing us to feel some degree of alignment with whatever potencies the plant carries. Calling to a saturnine plant will leave us with a very different feeling than calling to a venereal one. This residual potency is temporary, but can, at times, prove useful. Perhaps we wish to have a bit more acuity when conducting a tricky conversation. Calling to a mercurial plant spirit and offering the breath may help us to sharpen our communicative skills for a time. Likewise, a solar plant spirit may imbue us with more joyfulness and gratitude.

If your work with a particular plant spirit is fulfilling and very special to you, you may wish to form a closer and more trusting relationship. This spirit may, eventually, choose to become one of your guides or familiars, or you may simply cement your mutual admiration in the form of an agreement, or pact. This sort of bond is usually very long-term, so be sure you are quite serious before initiating it. The benefits are vast, though, since we will be able to call on the plant's spirit without its herb present, in any situation. It will, in effect, become a part of us on a deeper and more permanent level—a friend, guide, teacher, and protector to walk beside us on our path.

If such a bond is desirable to you, and if the spirit has given clear signs that it would be welcome, we should begin the next step with a formal invitation and an offering. It is a longstanding spiritual tradition to offer fumigation to spirits, and for good reason. Just as the spirit leaves the body, through either death or deliberate trance states, the smoke leaves the smoldering ash. What once existed in a bound physical form is released to twist and spread through the air, traveling and transforming. The fumigation is not merely pretty or pleasant to smell, but is deeply symbolic of the way the spirit, the thing we seek to conjure, is vaster and more potent than the physical form that is its temporary home. Keep in mind that, for our safety, we should always burn incense in a well-ventilated area.

The following method of plant spirit conjuration, designed with the intent of forming a close bond or a pact, is in fact a kind of *witch's almadel*, patterned after the famous Ars Almadel of the

Lemegeton, an old grimoiric operation that circulated among cunning folk and other magical practitioners hundreds of years ago. Originally, this method involved the construction of a wax square resting upon four candlesticks. Fumigation placed under the square would rise and ripple around its edges, acting as a medium for the perception of spirits. For the charmer or folk witch, however, this procedure can be simplified.

To Conjure the Plant Spirit

We can begin by placing the plant's gathered and dried herb into a vial or bottle. If the plant is not safe for you to touch, you can simply collect some soil from near where it grows. Just as charmers have long used graveyard dirt for spirit contact, the dirt from which a plant springs will contain enough of its spiritual potency to enable the connection, serving as a very fine substitute for the plant itself. Just take care to gather from the surface and some distance from the plant itself so as to avoid disturbing the root system.

Next, we will set an incense cone or a small amount of dried herbs alight within a small cauldron or old cast iron cooking pot, then hold or suspend the sacred vessel dedicated to the plant within the rising smoke. One can also purchase or design a small box, or perhaps a footstool, to sit over the incense—or even position the cleaned skull of an animal (always ethically sourced, of course) over a sturdy vessel containing a smoldering cone so that the smoke passes through the skull. Regardless of method, the operation is the same

- to suspend the plant's reliquary in the rising smoke, hallowing it for the spirit. Our goal is not to heat or burn the plant, but to allow the sweetly scented smoke to coil through and around its vessel, assuming new shapes that will communicate the spirit's will, and sanctifying its vessel as a sort of miniature temple.

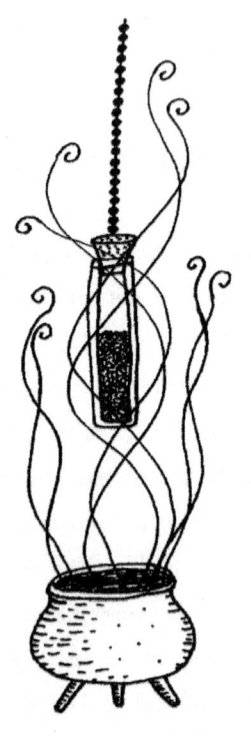

While the bottle or plant reliquary is suspended in the smoke, speak the words of conjuration. Consider turning to the examples of plant spirit invocations in the previous exercise, or write your own. The words can be the same as the ones you used when calling to the spirit less formally, or you can adapt a longer, more formal version for the work of conjuration. Either way, the tone of the incantation should be warm, welcoming, and should probably include some form of praise for the plant's powers and properties.

If our conjuration is successful, the movement of the smoke may begin to coil or straighten in a manner that is different from before. Feel free to ask questions, noting changes in the smoke's movement. We may also simply "feel" the presence of the spirit. If our witch-sight has become strong due to regular practice, we may perceive them. Images and impressions received from plant spirits are rarely humanoid in appearance, but are usually more amorphous. In my own perception of plant spirits, I've noticed that they are sometimes accompanied by lights or shrouded by strange darkness, which I cannot explain, except perhaps to wonder if it has some relationship with their processes of photosynthesis and the importance of light and darkness to their growth patterns.

In any event, it is at this stage that we can begin communication with the spirit, either relying on our powers of sight or through the use of some divinatory tool such as tarot or a pendulum. The goal is to discern some new and secret part of the spirit's nature so that we may form a relationship with it that is entirely our own. Most likely, any imagery, sounds, or impressions received will not make immediate sense. Accept them without trying to interpret or make sense of anything. Perceive these impressions for what they are: gifts to be accepted graciously.

After the spirit has been thanked for its presence and released warmly and politely, extinguish the incense, place the vessel carefully in a special place in your home, and record any images, feelings, sounds, utterances, or any other impressions with as much detail as possible, no matter how nonsensical they may seem. Note that we have not attempted to "seal" the spirit inside the vessel, nor will we. The spirit is not a pet or a slave, but a spiritual being that must enter into communion with us of its own volition. While spirit subjugation is a part of the craft many (though not all) of our ancestors practiced in the days of the grimoires, it is, perhaps, a tradition best remembered and not practiced, except in dire straits.

The communications received from the spirit can be used to interpret its names, seals, and even words of conjuration. Consider drawing out any images perceived, looking for key shapes that emerge. How might these lines and shapes fit together in a simplified form? Consider writing out the sounds you heard from the spirit. Read them forwards and backwards. How might these sounds string together into a kind of incantation? Consult the spirit seals of the *Clavicula Salomonis, Lemegeton, Black Pullet,* or other old grimoires for examples of how previous charmers interpreted spirit communications into images. How might the complex communication you received from this spirit be simplified into a form that can be used in this way? Keep in mind that the same spirit may have any number of names and seals, so there is no need to fret as if we were trying to empirically deduce the "one and only name" of this being. No such "name" exists. Just as different people in your life refer to you in various forms (Edgar, Ed, Mr. Richards, Sir, Father, Son, Brother, Nephew, Uncle, Colleague, Friend, Lover, Honey, Sweetheart, etc.), so does the spirit answer to a great many names in a great many aspects, as kaleidoscopic in its natures as any deity.

If all else fails, one can take a more structured approach to deciphering the spirit's name and seal. Though relying on the sight and intuition is preferable, it is possible to derive these details from the spirit using a common deck of playing cards. Cartomancy was a popular form of divination and spirit communication for previous generations, often more common than tarot since playing cards were more readily available until the 20th century.

A simple method to derive spirit names and other utterances entails assigning letters to the cards, then drawing them in sequence. In order to allow for the repetition of letters, which is a natural facet of language, we can use a model that assigns letter values to cards that are red (hearts and diamonds) and cards that are black (clubs and spades).

Red Cards

Ace	A
Two	B
Three	C
Four	D

Five	E
Six	F
Seven	G
Eight	H
Nine	I
Ten	J
Jack	K
Queen	L
King	M

Black Cards

Ace	N
Two	O
Three	P
Four	Q
Five	R
Six	S
Seven	T
Eight	U
Nine	V
Ten	W
Jack	X
Queen	Y
King	Z

Note that, even if performed carefully while conjuring the spirit, the sequence of letters can, at first, appear nonsensical. I recommend using what you know of this plant spirit's personality and qualities to assess the success of the operation. Often, the results form an anagram, which is a recognizable word hidden by the rearrangement of letters. Sometimes, a single letter is missing, the addition of which reveals the hidden name or password the spirit is attempting to communicate. While I find the intuitive adaptation of perceived sounds and utterances to be preferable, this method is reliable when other methods fall short.

But we must also consider the possibility that the sequence of drawn cards before us is not a name at all, but the makings of a seal; either the seal for more effectively conjuring the spirit itself, or a sigil for a particular charm or working that the spirit wishes to impart, that we might add it to our trove of charms at the ready. The derivation of seals is more easily accomplished with a square of cards, either nine cards (3 by 3) or sixteen cards (4 by 4). When we draw a line from the center of one card to the next, forming a sequence based on the assigned order of the cards, the result is a figure made of lines and angles.

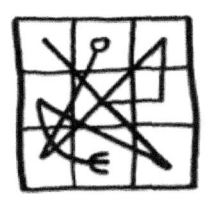

I recommend deciding on a clear order in advance, possibly hearts, then diamonds, then clubs, then spades, each suit naturally beginning with the Ace and ending with the King. The "line" of the seal then moves from the first in order to the last. Of course, it would be better to receive the spirit's revealed seal via our powers of sight and spiritual perception, intuitively arranging the images we are been granted, but if this proves difficult, the card-based method is a worthy substitute.

Once the spirit's gifts have been deciphered, one can decorate the spirit vessel with them, or one can simply record and keep them in a personal grimoire. These keys can be used to conjure the spirit once more, again holding the vessel above the fumigation, this time with the spirit's seal inscribed on the floor in chalk, traced on the air with the finger, or simply held in the mind's eye while chanting its received name. The meticulous circles and orations of previous ages are unnecessary for us now, for we have formed a bond with this spirit, and it has chosen to share space with us. We can now announce our desire to adopt this spirit as a familiar or guide, perhaps cementing the deal with a pact made and signed on a bit of paper to be stored in the same vessel or in our grimoire.

Once the bond is made, our perception of the spirit will become clearer and more vivid over time, and we will be able to conjure it into our presence with little more than a focused word, thought, or gesture. This is possible not because we have "mastered" the spirit in any way, but because we have formed a bond tempered with love and care. If we tend to this bond carefully, remembering to offer incense, breath, and/or words of love and gratitude regularly, it will only grow stronger over the years. The spirit becomes both a partner in the craft and a teacher, able to impart new charms and offer keys to our progress on the path over time.

Occult Botanical Keys and Maps

While it is certainly enough to understand the magical properties of plants as being akin to personalities, there are in fact many ways of understanding and categorizing the qualities of our green friends. When outlined together, these qualities form a kind of map that is useful to us, for it illustrates more clearly the relationships between plants and affords us an understanding of how they might fit together into interdependent systems.

The "planets" of classical astrology include the Sun, Moon, Mars, Mercury, Jupiter, Venus, and Saturn. Although these are not technically "stars" by modern scientific standards (with the exception of the Sun), these were generally referred to as "the wandering stars" up until the 1600s—the Moon, of course, being an exception that was still included as a category of magical associations due to its similar, though unique influence. Each of these heavenly bodies carries a wealth of mysteries and mythology, and it is worth taking a moment to unpack them here in their natural pairings, which reveal more about their natures.

Pairing One: Sun and Moon. The Sun is usually associated with wholeness, wholesome joys, activity or work, healing, and states of being that we might call "fulfilled" or "balanced." Solar herbs have been used magically to bring joy and wholeness, fulfillment, and conventional forms of happiness to do with family and work. Conversely, the Moon is associated with ecstasies and dreaming, intoxication, inspiration, and sleep, but also madness and the loss of control. Lunar herbs have been used magically for prophecy and divination, to bring rest, to inspire dreams or visions, but also to loosen our desire to assert control, to encourage us to step outside of what is familiar and comfortable. We can think of this dynamic as speaking to the "known" and "unknown," since the light of the Sun and Moon facilitate two realities around us: one clear, knowable, and wholesome; the other dark, secretive, and thrilling.

Pairing Two: Jupiter and Saturn. Jupiter is usually associated with leadership, order, power, authority, and constructive progress towards the achievement of goals. It is also associated with fertility and with the growth of one's business or projects. (Think of Zeus and his many legendary offspring of various mothers.) The potency of Jupiter is often used for legal favor, matters of authority and leadership, and of course fertility. On the other side of this dynamic, Saturn embodies a potency of destruction and release, being associated with death and the world of the dead. Its potency is often used for curses, hexes, and necromancy (communication with the dead). Interestingly, this "wandering star" also distills its own otherworldly form of fertility and growth, for it signifies the growth and advancement of the otherworldly body in its own domain. This dynamic is similar to a tree growing both below and above the surface. Above the soil line, we see the fertility of Jupiter, but what is unseen below, in the vast network of roots working quietly in the dark, is the fertility of Saturn.

Pairing Three: Mars and Venus. Mars has, since classical times, been associated with war, violence, and conquest. It is no surprise, then, that the potency of Mars is combative and aggressive, being well-suited to protective charms and lesser curse-work, but also to matters of success in overcoming obstacles. Conversely, Venus is often associated with love, beauty, and pleasures, and its potency is often used in charms of love and attraction, but also in matters of self-care, confidence, and self-love or self-esteem. The polarity between these two stars is not quite so simple as "male and female," as the old texts have suggested, but instead lies in forms of connection and disconnection with others. Mars seeks to dominate, which is not always evil, but sometimes necessary in order to contain the harm a person wishes to do. Venus seeks to endear, which is not always good, for the goals of this work can be manipulative and *venomous* (a word, in fact, derived from the same root as *Venus*).

Mercury is interesting here, as it is the only wandering star that is not part of a pairing or binary. Its symbol captures its mixed nature, being that of a horned Venus, sometimes associated with the old horned deities and with the folkloric witches' Devil (a figure distinct from the Christian devil). These horned figures of classical mythology were a mixture of man and beast, belonging to two worlds at once. Similarly, Mercury's potency often entails the crossing of boundaries, be they spiritual, material, or interpersonal. This star is called upon in matters of communication, financial exchange, travel, and passage between worlds.

The seven planets together form either a hexagram or an asteriskos, both being ancient magical symbols connected with stars and the convergence of planes of reality. When mapped out visually, we can see these pairings of forces balance each other: Sun and Moon, Jupiter and Saturn, Mars and Venus.

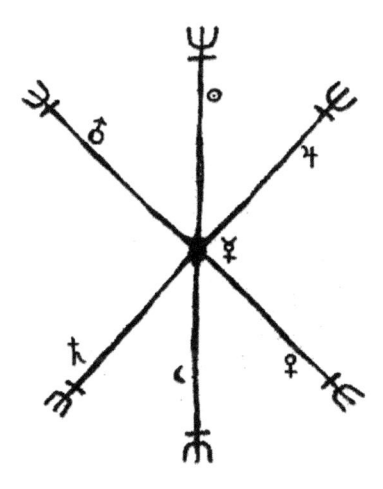

Because Mercury's very nature has to do with shifting and mixture, it is often placed at the center of such models. (This is obviously

not a model of the solar system, so we need not feel odd about this placement.)

This layout is helpful when dissecting a plant's nature for several reasons. If the plant is possessed of both lunar and solar qualities, we can say that it contains a convergence or dichotomy in its potencies. These sorts of plants, like the two-faced Janus, may contain powers to do with opening hidden doors, keeping gates between worlds, or acting as an initiator, which is to say, a spirit that teaches and confers spiritual power to human charmers.

We can further interpret the proximity of potencies on such maps to determine plants that are adjacent to one another, indicating that they are in some way similar or allied. Martial herbs are thus allied by solar and saturnine herbs, sharing some similarities with their natures. Lunar herbs share certain qualities with both venereal and saturnine herbs. This is useful knowledge, for if we do not have access to three lunar herbs utilize together when creating a planetary essence or other preparation, we can draw on one lunar, one venereal, and one saturnine herb as a worthy replacement for three lunar ones.

If this same field of wandering stars is conveyed as a hexagram, we can see the clear convergence of two triangles, each made up of three planets. Thus, the Moon, Jupiter, and Mars are connected in the downward-pointing triangle. The Sun, Saturn, and Venus are contained in the upward-pointing one. If adjacent planets on the previous model describe similarity between planets, then these trinaries illustrate tenser relationships between bodies that together form a kind of balance. The Moon, then, would have a tense relationship with mars and Jupiter, which makes sense when considering their natures. We can think of these potencies as "balancing" the others belonging to its trinary.

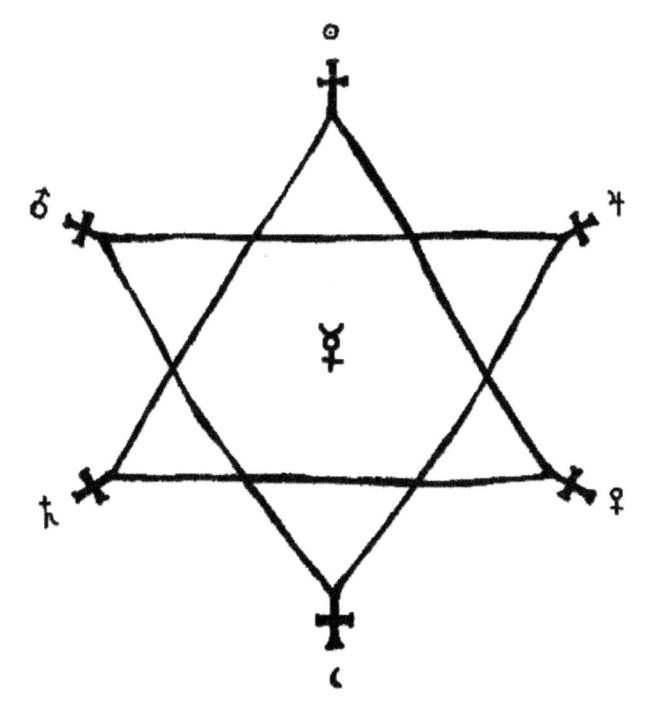

Thus, if a magical working requires combating the target's delusion and narcissism, Saturn or the Sun would be excellent potencies to select, for they naturally "balance out" the force of Venus that is the root of the issue in a way that is gentler than Mars would be able to accomplish.

As you explore and discover how your own local flora fit together in a system or structure of magical potencies, be mindful not to get lost in the process. It is better to know intimately the personality of a handful of plants than to blindly and reductively categorize hundreds of them. The task is simply too big to do it well, and the fruit of this labor is like the horizon, receding as we approach it. The more time we spend "assigning" designations to these living beings, the more obfuscated their complex personalities become to us, erecting a kind of wall before us (the dreaded "wall of correspondences") that *seems* to offer a window into understanding plants, but in fact, does the opposite by oversimplifying their natures. The point is not to squish as many varieties of flora as possible into little boxes of meaning, but to identify *some* useful aspects of a *small* number of plants that are available to us in our own lives.

To this end, one useful practice is noting local plant cycles alongside festivals or sabbat dates, marking the seasons with the plants that flower at that time of the year. This is, of course, nothing new. Older generations would name the series of frosts in early spring after the plants that flourished thereafter (hence "blackberry winter," "dogwood winter," "redbud winter," and many other names for frosts preserved in Appalachia and elsewhere in the world). Most of us readily associate holly and mistletoe with the Yuletide season, while apples and squash are associated with All Hallows' Eve. Notice, though, the less ostentatious plants around you at key times of the year. Perhaps the violets of early spring or the mugwort ready to flower by midsummer. What do these plant spirits reveal about the magical tide at hand? Working with these plants at these times can be a kind of sabbat rite, a way of honoring the season by honoring a plant spirit that reaches out to us during that certain time of year.

Of course, in our endless wealth of innovation, sharp witches the world over have discovered a variety of mappings to illustrate the relationships between the powers of plant spirits. One need not look far to find the categorization of plant potencies based on the astrological signs of the zodiac or even the letters of the runic alphabet.

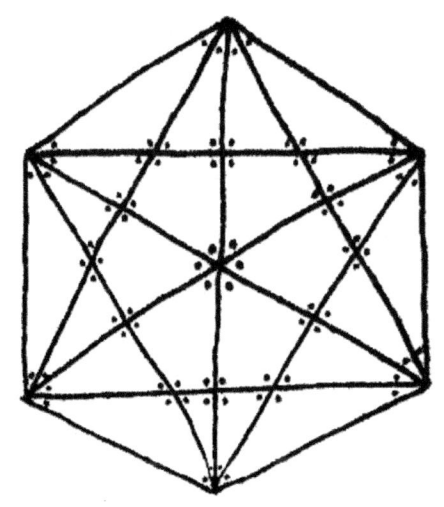

One could, conceivably, discover any such map of plant potencies by visually diagramming magical elements at work in one's own practice, so it is worth experimenting in order to discover your own in addition to these. Although the magical ontology known as the hermetic qabalah is the most well-known example, it is, in fact, only one example out of many such "maps" derived from magical experience and practice. The lines and intersections formed by connecting the seven points of the planetary star are worthy of study on their own as a way of "mapping" relationships between magical potencies.

What matters is taking the time to contemplate the relationships between plants and how the forces at work within their spirits relate to one another, as this understanding brings us to a deeper level in our practice, not just in magical herbalism, but in our witchcraft as a whole. Consider recording one or more useful plant potency maps in your personal grimoire so that you may refer to it over the course of your practice.

Charming with Herbs

Herbal magic need not be overly ornate or ceremonial. Once we have taken the time to observe and understand a plant, noting its potencies and making contact with its spirit, we are already equipped with the keys to success. What remains is to call the potency we require from the appropriate plant spirits, creating from them an herbal preparation that can be used in a variety of ways in our craft.

This effectiveness of a prepared formulation crafted from the potencies dwelling with plants relies on the folk-magical principle of *contagion*, which is to say, the transference of magical effects by nearness or proximity. Our herbal preparation, be it an oil, an essence, or a sachet, will imbue its target with the desired magical effect because it has been in close contact with them. The poppet functions a bit differently, since it is, itself, a *simulacrum* or creature of sympathy, designed to simulate the person who is the target of the working. Even in this case, though, the principle of contagion is at work, for the magical effects are transferred via actions taken on or objects placed nearby the poppet itself.

Regardless of the formula, the ritual process can look quite similar, though witches often develop their own preferences over time for certain recipes. In general, I think of this process as having four steps:

1. A simple opening rite.
2. Calling to the spirit within the plant.
3. Crafting the preparation itself.
4. Consecrating the preparation for its intended purpose.

Other witches working within Wicca or other traditions may prefer to cast a circle or observe certain rituals specific to their vein of craft, but for myself and many other folk practitioners, the old methods used by our ancestors are much simpler and require little fuss. (This is at least true on the surface; the Devil is in the details, as they say).

Consider reading through the following paragraphs for a glimpse of what my own process looks like, but do consider adapting your own version in your personal grimoire for easy reference.

The Opening Rite

The opening rites I love best for this work are not tedious or exhausting, but simple. I often simply light a candle and rely on an old standard incantation of Scottish origin:

> *Kindle now a fire bright*
> *With our Lady in its light.*
> *Upon the ceiling and the floor,*
> *On every wall and every door.*

This is my own adaptation, but another version of this charm appears in the *Carmina Gadelica*, a beloved collection of early modern charms. The "Lady" referred to in this charm appears variously in other, similar incantations as Mary or Brigid, and this is both a truth and a veil. This type of opening rite calls upon a greater spirit related to one's connection to the craft, and it would be wise to consider carefully which old spirits, gods, or saints you are connected to already.

Otherwise, in the absence of some more specific opening rite of your own, we can always rely on the *caim*, which is a charm upon the space around us. The caim (pronounced "key-ehm"), which is Celtic in origin, appears in many iterations, but my own version is this:

> *Before me,*
> *Behind me,*
> *Above me,*
> *Below me,*
> *On my right hand,*
> *On my left hand,*

I conjure thee, o ring of art.

The principle at work in this charm is the calling of a force surrounding the practitioner, setting a space between worlds and amplifying magical acts. This is probably the closest thing in my craft practice to the magical circle used in Wicca, but it appears as recently as the 1800s as a kind of walking prayer, a way of shifting one's spiritual consciousness in the space surrounding the practitioner.

If a working is saturnine or martial in nature, or if it entails what we might call malefic or baneful craft, or if I simply feel it is "right," I might use a conjuration of the crossroads, establishing a fulcrum point where worlds converge:

> *One, two, three, and four.*
> *The Old One knocks upon the door.*
> *Welcome him from floor to roof.*
> *Drink to him in a horse's hoof.*
> *Call the cat, the toad, the bran.*
> *Come to the feast, all ye who can.*
> *One, two, three, and four.*
> *The Old One is here, so no more.*

Make no mistake that the "Old One" in the incantation above is the folkloric Devil, though I am sometimes fond of saying "Old Ones" in order to differentiate between the many spirits who have been given this title over the course of history (often unfairly and not of their own choosing). One old version of this charm appears in Welsh witch-lore. In this working, it is sometimes helpful to mark the space beneath or above the candle with the asteriskos or three-lined star in order to consecrate the point of convergence between worlds.

For your own practice, utilize any of these methods, or none at all. Call to your ancestors, or perhaps call to the land, sea, and sky. Call to your own spirit, your own witch-self if you desire. What matters is that one takes a moment to situate oneself, to remember that you are a being straddling worlds, that your consciousness is flexible, that you exist both in this world and the otherworld. Do whatever it takes for you to achieve that "feeling of otherness" that you achieved in the ekstasis exercises previously. Without that feeling, our words are merely words, our actions are merely actions, and our charms are empty things entirely.

Calling to the Spirit

The process of calling to or waking the plant spirit within the readied ingredients can be as simple or elaborate as one wishes. See the previous examples of this process on pages 63-64 for a refresher. The central point here is to call out to the potency that has perhaps grown dormant in the plant matter one is using. We do this so that the magical properties in the leaves (or flowers, roots, or what have you) are quickened and vital before preparing the formula at hand.

If the herbs are freshly gathered and the spirit was already called while doing so, there is usually no need to do so again. This process is, however, especially important when working with dried herbs shipped and sold in stores or online, since these plants have been desecrated by the processes of mechanical farming, packaging, and shipping. Hallowing the leaves or roots of these plants again can remind them of their sacred potencies, awakening what has grown dormant in the herbal material.

Crafting the Preparation

Care should be taken in selecting one or more herbs related to the magical goal. I find that there are two methods for approaching this work: enhancing and balancing. When we select an herb that will *bring* some needed magical force, we are *enhancing*. Conversely, when we select an herb that will *ward off* or *negate* some other undesired element at work, we are *balancing*. This latter approach is useful when we find ourselves consumed by a problem that encompasses all of our thoughts and energies.

Although it is more popular in modern witchcraft to use banishing work in which a certain spirit, energy, or person is cast out from one's life, I find that this approach sometimes creates more problems than it solves. All things in nature exist for a purpose, even if we do not understand that purpose at the time. A house, for example, may have mice, but burning down the house is a terrible solution to the problem. A balancing approach would be to adopt a cat instead. Our feline friend will enjoy hunting mice for us, and we will be free from worry without resorting to destruction in the process. A balancing approach to the craft is like this. We can call in spirits and potencies that will mitigate the issue for us and restore balance rather than attacking every problem with fire and brimstone.

If we work with one herb alone, we are calling in the spirit of that plant in one or more of its aspects. We can specify which aspect during the consecration process. This type of preparation may be called an "Oil of Mugwort," "Essence of Mint," or "Balm of Chamomile." If we select multiple herbs that share a planetary potency, we are crafting a planetary preparation, imbued with the force of that planet's magical qualities. Such a preparation might be called a "Vinegar of Saturn" or "Sachet of Jupiter." We might also select multiple herbs that share a common folkloric thread or other, more subtle magical signature, and assign the preparation a given purpose during the consecration stage. This might result in more specific formulas, such as an "Incense of Prosperity" or "Powder of Punishment."

Consult the recipes in the next section after this one for specific formulations towards a variety of goals:

✝ Essences are usually imbibed, mixed into drink and food, or added to bathwater. Infusions and tinctures can be used similarly, but may not be as safe, depending on the herb. (We can always substitute using the spirit water, oil, vinegar, and salt formulas if an herb is not safe to consume.)

✠ Vinegars are often used for washing and cleansing doorways, windows, porches, floors, or other places around one's home.

✠ Oils can be used to dress candles, talismans, or anoint the pulse points (temples, neck, and wrists), or they may be added to bathwater.

✠ Ointments, salves, and balms (these three unguents differing only by degree of firmness) are likewise used to anoint, but with the added preservative of beeswax, which creates a more solid, less messy result.

✠ Powders and salts are usually blown onto a porch, an object, or laid in a line on personal property. Salts can also be added to bathwater.

✠ Incense may be prepared from an herb (if safe to burn) in order to distribute its potency into a human space via smoke.

✠ Inks may be used in the drawing of sigils, in written incantations, and in the commitment of spirit contracts (or written pacts) to paper.

✠ Talismans in the form of dried plant matter, sachets, witch's bottles, and the "plant-veiled stone" may be carried on the person in order to impart a given spiritual potency around one's person.

✠ Relics in the form of braided dollies, strung berries, or

dried roots provide a vessel for housing the spirit in one's home or place of work, acting as a miniature temple to a particular plant spirit.

✠ Plant spirit water, oils, vinegars, salts, powders, etc., are powerful formulations used to a variety of ends. These carry the plant's magical potency without any actual plant matter, making these formulas an ideal approach to working with herbs that are unsafe for us to consume or plants which are endangered and should not be gathered.

Consecration

To consecrate, sanctify, or hallow something is to make it sacred, but more than that, this magical process gives our herbal preparation a clear directive. We consecrate things *for a clearly defined purpose*. Sometimes, this purpose is quite broad, such as an oil consecrated to draw in the potencies of Venus. At other times, this purpose can be distinct, such as an essence consecrated to endear the user to persons in authority. Be decisive about the goals and purpose of the formula, recognizing that one herbal preparation simply cannot do or be everything at once. A focused will with a single goal is like the point of a sharp thorn; a confused will, drawn in too many directions at once, is like straw blown in the wind.

On a related note, we must also recognize that real magic, the kind practiced by charmers throughout history, does not defy the laws of physics, but must work within them. Consecrating a vinegar with the purpose of turning objects into gold may not be the best use of one's magical effort, but an unguent that brings prosperity might very well be, for we have given our formulation, which is an embodiment of the potency of one or more plant spirits, a task (prosperity) that may be accomplished in whatever way it deems practical and appropriate. In short, no one likes being tasked with the impossible, so when consecrating an herbal preparation, do be reasonable.

My own process of consecration in my craft is very simple, usually drawing on the language of the Solomonic grimoires, which tend to address various implements of craft as *creatures*. I am fond of this verbiage because it emphasizes the crafted formulation as a sort of living magical being:

> *I conjure thee, creature of <u>oil</u> and <u>mugwort</u>,*
> *Under the dominion of the <u>Moon</u>,*
> *<u>To hold the potency of spiritual sight and journeying</u>,*
> *And under the dominion of <u>Mars</u>,*
> *<u>To guard the journeyer at the threshold</u>*
> *In our Lady's name.*

As you can see, the underlined words and phrases above can be altered, preserving the verbal formula and manner of address while changing out the ingredients (here, oil and mugwort), the planetary influences (here, the Moon and Mars), and the task specific to the consecration. "In our Lady's name" is another general call to Mary or Brigid, but also to other, veiled entities that are connected to these figures. Have no qualms about substituting the name or title of another spirit you work with. In the absence of any, one can always call to one's ancestors, guides, or familiars—or simply to the land, sea, and sky. Do not be afraid to tinker with old charms. They are, after all, the result of hundreds of years of tinkering. The old craft does not come to us via a purist's preservation efforts, but rather, through centuries of experimentation and adaptation. Remember that witchcraft is a living thing, and allow yourself room to grow in your own direction.

I typically utilize either a candle or a small vessel of burning incense to consecrate an object while I speak the conjuration. For a potent consecration, I hold the herbal preparation in my hand in the same manner as the witch's almadel, suspended in the rising coils of incense. At other times, I prefer to simply hold it a safe distance above a lit candle, feeling the rising warmth. Both smoke and candleflame embody a kind of agency and unpredictability in their movements, and for this reason, they have both long signified the presence and movement of spirit. The smoke of the extinguished candle, in my practice, signifies the charm spreading through the air to achieve its target, and so holding the herbal preparation in this smoke as it rises can achieve a similar effect to incense fumigation, though with less drama.

The consecrated oil or essence (or what have you) is only complete, of course, when it "feels right." There should be a sense of satisfaction and "doneness" that is difficult to describe in words, but can very clearly be felt in practice. If this isn't achieved, look over your process, and make tweaks to anything that didn't feel quite right. Since we have made contact with the plant spirit and learned from the plant itself, we can trust our intuition at this stage and adjust as necessary.

When you are ready and satisfied, consider labeling your preparation with a clear name and date. A tincture of chickweed would simply be called "Tincture of Chickweed." An oil of three herbs designed to draw in the potencies of Mercury would simply be called "Oil of Mercury." An essence of various flowers and leaves designed to help one find new love might be called "Essence of Sweetheart." I'm fond of simply using masking tape or craft tape to label bottles, jars, and vials. If you cut the tape cleanly with a pair of scissors instead of tearing, the resulting label looks quite neat and is far less expensive than the various stickers one can buy. It also sticks very well and can be removed later without much fuss when the bottle is empty and ready for cleaning and reuse.

Once you have developed confidence in the basic ritual formula above, I recommend experimentation. Witches are always experimenting with recipes and ritual formulas, simplifying what feels too ornate, removing what feels ineffective, and introducing new elements into our practice based on feeling and intuition. We can also enrich our practice by incorporating the folklore of our region and our ancestry. The greatest troves of magical wisdom often hide behind what are called today *superstitions*. Consider, as a source of ritual and spellcraft, the act of blowing dandelion seeds on the wind, or the gathering of a "lucky" seed to be kept in the pocket. How can these traditions be elevated with the intentionality and grace of simple ritual? Use the framework from before, but feel free to adapt and change it as necessary. Look to the old wives' tales of your grandparents or great grandparents and to the plants around you. Weave the old into the new, so that it may be honored and preserved in your craft. Consider that the old superstitions are *already rituals*, simplified and ingrained in popular sayings and nursery rhymes in order to be carried on the currents of time across generations, perhaps so that some clever charmer might one day uncover their secret potential.

However you approach your charm work, remember that the secret to ritual effectiveness usually lies not in ornament, but in *simplicity*. When I was new to my magical practice, I often felt the urge to incorporate as many bells and whistles as possible, that I must, somehow, infuse gravitas into ritual through theatrics. While there is something to be said for the spectacle of ritual, this is not, ultimately, where potency comes from. Don't be afraid to grow more casual in your charm work over time. Like the experienced hands of a cook who has prepared the meal many times before, we learn how to arrive at the moment of potency more efficiently over time. The important thing is to follow the feeling rather than the trappings of ritual. Perform the charm carefully and ceremonially the first time to get the flavor of the thing, then give yourself permission to play with what makes it "tick."

Inevitably, at some point in one's craft, we come to the question of how best to use our gifts. Magical ethics can be quite a complex topic in folk witchery. In some modern traditions of craft, there are firm rules regarding ethics in magical practice, the "threefold law" of Wicca being the most famous example. Most wiccans believe that what is cast comes back upon the caster. For the folk witch, and for most traditional witches, however, no such rules exist. Our ancestors were skilly folk and cunning folk, herb doctors and fairy doctors, and they cursed with one hand and blessed with the other, trusting their intuition and considering the context of each situation carefully. Like any creature in the wild, the folk witch is capable of kindness towards loved ones and malice towards enemies, and among folk and traditional charmers, this is largely viewed as natural.

That said, there is some wisdom in choosing one's battles, I think. While I haven't experienced a "magical rebound effect" as described by some, working baneful craft does come with a kind of price—or rather, certain side effects. These aren't entirely negative, but should be considered carefully. In my experience, magic passes *through* the practitioner, and just like any other vessel, a portion of what is passed through us lingers there. Working malefic charms routinely may bring you closer to spirits that are dark in nature. (*Dark* is not the same as *evil*, mind you, and these spirits are sometimes wise and generous in their own ways, but can admittedly be fearsome.) In daily life, we may feel a bit freer with our speech and actions, less restrained and inhibited by propriety. This, too, is neither good nor bad, but can be a noticeable change to one's personality. Ultimately, I believe that so-called "black magic" brings us closer in communion with dark spirits and changes our nature in subtle ways, making us more like these entities, which are neither evil nor demonic, but simply have a perspective that is different from beings described as "light" or "benevolent." These two sides to our art are sometimes described as "dextral" and "sinistral," like the right and left hand, respectively; the implication, of course, being that each of us possesses both.

More importantly, we should consider carefully the effects of our workings simply because *we wish to be kind*. The folk witch usually operates with kindness—both towards the human world and the spirit world—not because we are afraid of punishment, but because *we care about others*. Just as we do not condemn the spider or the serpent for acting in its nature, so too should we recognize that human nature is varied and complex. Perhaps a friend has asked for a curse on an ex in order to punish their infidelity. Do we trust this friend to give us the whole story? The story of treachery and hurt brought before us might simply be what they wish us to hear, or it might be limited by what they are able to perceive about the situation. How would a curse help this situation? Would the satisfaction of the victim's suffering be worth the pain of regret when we change our minds, when we find that the curse has gone too far? Would it not be simpler for the wounded party to accept that this person is *acting in their nature*, and move on? Could craft designed to help them heal and seek out their own joy be more useful, in this moment, than the momentary satisfaction of a curse?

Ultimately, I make no judgment regarding other witches' personal ethics. In fact, I believe some curses can be just and helpful. My only wish for you, dear reader, is that you never have to regret your actions, so do consider carefully *what you really want* before drawing on your craft in pursuit of any goal. Sometimes our desires are fleeting, changing from moment to moment. Understanding ourselves and our true desires is one of the most difficult aspects of this path, but our cumulative acts over the course of years define who we are. Decide now what sort of practitioner you would like to be, and choose actions that will bring you closer to the sort of charmer you wish to become.

Riding Plants

Witchcraft is, at its core, a form of animist spiritual practice, and one of the hallmarks of animism has always been the otherworldly journey. The practice of leaving the body in spirit form in order to travel between worlds is neither fictitious nor supernatural, but quite commonplace in indigenous cultures throughout the world. When we say *witchcraft*, what we often mean is *the collective memory of our animist-pagan roots*, even if those roots are hidden beneath hundreds of years of denial. People in first-world countries are sometimes fond of fetishizing animist practices in indigenous cultures, buying factory produced voodoo dolls in gift shops or making memes out of spirit animals. Similar, but distinct practices were alive in pre-Christian Europe as well, and the memory of them survived and re-emerged as a kind of collective nightmare of self-loathing in the witch-lore of the early modern period.

Even today, in North America and much of Europe, animism is viewed as somehow "primitive," when really, it is deeply human and intrinsic to our nature. We give names to rivers, mountains, and lakes. We say things like, "those clouds look angry" or "that briar snagged me." We refer to our houses—and sometimes, old, beloved trees—as "she." We set out offerings of seed for songbirds and nectar for hummingbirds. We entrust our wishes to ladybugs, crickets, and stars in the sky. And perhaps most importantly of all, we *dream*, and we speak of our dreaming in the terms of lived experiences. "I was wading in the river, and then I grew wings and flew into the sky," we might say, or, "You and I were on a trip together, but I can't remember where." Sometimes, inexplicably, the other person dreamt of us as well, though they can't recall the details. Sometimes, we come upon a meadow or a field in our waking life that feels so familiar, and we cannot shake the feeling that we have visited before, as if it happened in another world—a world much like this one, but somehow not.

Witch-flight as it is practiced today is an ecstatic experience that is accomplished in many different ways. Some have described it as a form of self-induced trance, which is probably not inaccurate, but also somehow not quite right. Others have described it as a hallucination or daydream. Again, these are not exactly inaccurate, for some witches do choose to use substances to achieve flight, and it *can* sometimes feel like a sort of waking dream, but for me, these descriptions aren't quite right either. Many witches do not rely on substances to achieve their flight, and the experience of it is more vivid and profound than a mere daydream. Spirit flight has also been described, in New Age circles, as merely another form of pathworking or astral projection. This isn't quite right either, for pathworking involves traveling along a pre-programmed course of memorized experiences, and astral projection involves traveling the "astral realm," which is distinct from the complex, unpredictable cosmology of the otherworld.

What none of these descriptions capture about the flight of the spirit is that it is somehow *pleasurable* in a way that is difficult to describe. It feels like a loosening or an untethering of sorts. It is also wildly unpredictable in its cosmology, terrains, and experiences. Even visiting areas that are quite mundane in our waking lives can reveal things we did not expect to encounter. The beings of the otherworld—whether we call them the fae, the spirits of the dead, or simply "spirits"—might react to us in any number of ways. For witches new to the experience, it is often helpful to first approach a friendly, familiar tree, pond, stream, or hill to serve as a guide or helper. Fortunately, if we have made contact with the plant spirit, one such guide is already available to us.

One famous saying from Scottish lore, "as rank a witch as ever rode ragwort," preserves a key. Witches and faeries—who are in many stands of lore closely related—have long been said to "ride plants." This has been frequently misinterpreted to imply that the "riders" must be diminutive in stature, capable of straddling the stem of a plant, but most of the old faery lore implies that these beings were of similar size and build to humans of their time. Instead, we should read the folklore surrounding the riding of plants as a poetic way of saying *to travel with the plant's aid*. This aligns quite cleanly with early modern witch-lore, as witches were once said to receive a special stick that would itself transport them to their revels, usually as a gift from the witches' Devil—a figure related to faery lore and distinct from the biblical character.

The famous "flying ointment" of medieval and early modern lore was said to have been used by witches to transport them over great distances, leaving their sleeping bodies behind. While the famed ingredients of henbane, thornapple, deadly nightshade, mandrake, and other psychoactive plants were certainly known to have brought about altered states of consciousness, they are also well-known poisons. In many of these tales, the purpose of the flight in question was to harm or wound the spirits of others, and so it makes sense that the practitioner would "dress herself" with poison, calling on a baneful plant spirit to aid this type of flight. The truth is that witches can "ride" *any plant they choose*, so long as they possess the skill to do so. An oil or ointment prepared from a safe plant will work just as well if the approach is careful and well-planned. What's more, the plant we choose to aid us on our journey can color the journey itself, revealing otherworldly keys along the way that are unique and obtainable only through riding with the aid of that particular plant spirit. If a given plant is unsafe for you to use in unguent form, turn to the plant spirit oil formula provided on pages 146-149. These formulas are magically imbued with the plant's potencies, but contain no actual plant matter.

I sometimes hear from practitioners new to the arts of transvection (or spirit flight) who tell me that the process feels difficult for them. They usually say that they have spent countless hours focusing and straining, trying to will their spirit to leave their body, but to no avail. While it may seem that we must *will* the spirit to vacate the body in order to meet success in our endeavor, the truth is quite the opposite. Ecstasy and release do not arrive through force, but through *surrender*. It takes an enormous amount of focus and energy to hold the spirit in the body, especially for those with a great deal of natural skill or experience in spirit work. Witches—and in fact, charmers of all kinds—are possessed of two natures: the mundane self that drives to work, shops for groceries, takes out the recycling, and generally meets the complex demands of human life in modern society; and the other self—the dark and wild spirit within, which we must, in some ways, restrain and seal away in order to function in daily life. Learning how to "unclench" the hidden muscle and release this inner nature is intuitive for some, but more difficult for others. (Interestingly, queer and trans individuals—and others who have had to consciously hide parts of themselves in daily life—seem to be especially gifted at achieving the release necessary for flight.) No amount of concentration or willpower will "force" the ecstatic state to arrive. Instead, we must surrender to it, much like taking off our clothes and slipping into a warm bath. The self we seek to free is not somewhere else, but here. It has already arrived. To free it, we need only remove the shackles.

If you have not had much success yet with conjuring the spirit of the plant, do return to those exercises before attempting flight, as the one builds upon the foundation of the other. After beginning with the awakening of the sight and spirit conjuration processes found on pages 55-56 and 67-70, respectively, take up the prepared oil or unguent of your chosen plant (being sure it is safe for you to use), and attempt the following:

Spirit Flight via Unguent

✠ Choose a dark, quiet room in which to begin, lit by a single candle. Darkness and quiet are important to this process.

✠ If you wish, begin with a simple incantation, perhaps the following, which is derived from the preserved charms of famed witch Isobel Gowdie:

> *Through the hidden door I go*
> *To learn of what no man may know,*
> *And I shall go in Our Lady's name*
> *Until I come home again.*

Do feel free to change out "Our Lady's name" for "the Devil's name," depending on your preferences. The latter would be more aligned with Dame Gowdie's own approach.

✠ Begin applying your magically crafted formula to your skin in smooth, rhythmic motions, perhaps beginning with your arms. Slide one hand up and down the inside of the forearm, then alternate to the other. Let these motions flow in rhythm with your breath.

- Maintaining rhythmic strokes, move on to your neck and temples. Some witches seem to have success with their feet as well. Focus on enjoying this process, and let your intuition guide your hands. Just avoid sensitive areas.
- Let the experience of applying the unguent become a kind of self-massage, and as your consciousness begins to loosen and relax, allow the feeling of release to rise within you as before in the previous exercises. With the movement of your hands across your own skin, it should feel as if you are sloughing away a costume, a self that is not needed in this moment, allowing your witch-self to emerge, like a serpent shedding its skin.
- Once you feel the "loosening" of the ecstatic state coming to fruition, cup your oiled hands about your face, and breathe in the essence of the plant therein. (Here is another reason to choose a safe plant.) Allow yourself to be consumed by the plant's essence, to soak in it.
- While you are breathing from your cupped hands, turn your attention to the space about you using your witch-sight. You will likely perceive the plant spirit there (if not all around you).
- Explore the area around you in spirit form. If you are indoors, a window will likely serve as the entrance point for your journey. If outside, allow your consciousness to slide through the roots of a nearby tree, a hole in the ground, an unseen tunnel, or even into a body of water.
- The visions that come on the journey that follows are meant for you and you alone. To end your flight, simply alert the plant spirit

that you wish to return to your body. (It may sense this need before you do.) Make your way home, returning along the same path you journeyed (you will sense it quite easily with the plant spirit's help), working backwards towards your body, which is waiting for you.

✠ If you feel afraid at any point and wish to return to your body quickly, simply slap your palms firmly against the ground, your thighs, or the surface of a table (mindful of candles or incense). You can also use the phrase *rentum tormentum*, a reliable incantation of return, once again left to us by Dame Gowdie.

Note that there are many ways to use spirit flight in one's practice. The exhilaration of the experience is reason enough, but this regular exercise also sharpens the sight and enables us to more easily perceive otherworldly spirits and currents in our daily life. One might choose to visit a loved one in order to offer blessings performed in spirit form. One might also visit a nearby tree or body of water in order to communicate with a spirit there. Traveling to a place that is a source of stress can sometimes reveal a solution to a vexing problem via signs or messages from spirits. The possibilities are quite endless. Famously, witches can, if they choose, pay a visit to an enemy in order to torment them, but I don't recommend this practice, dear reader. If the target is gifted themselves, or if they are guarded by their own familiars, guides, or ancestors, you may be in for a nasty reception indeed. If they are *very* gifted, they can even do lasting harm to your spirit body, which can be very difficult to heal.

One of the most ancient methods for attaining spirit flight is via dreaming, for it is in dreams that we are most easily able to cross into the otherworld and interact with spirits. Many plants associated with dreaming and divination—and most plants possessing lunar or saturnine potencies—are capable of aiding in this process. Depending on the safety of the plant, we might ingest three drops of either the plant's spirit water or flower/leaf essence prior to retiring in the evening, accompanied by a simple ritual:

Dream Flight via Potion

✠ Before retiring to bed, find a quiet, dark place in which to light a single candle.

✠ Hold the vial before you so that the light from the candle passes through its liquid, and if you wish, speak a brief incantation to the spirit within, such as the following charm, adapted from the preserved folk ballad called *Nottamun Town*:

> *Come a stone horse, and come a stone mare,*
> *Gray mane, gray tail, gray stripe down her back.*
> *From saddle to stirrup, I'll mount ye again,*
> *And on my ten toes, I'll ride over the plain.*

✠ Take three drops of your chosen preparation upon the tongue. Remember that spirit water is a wise choice if a plant is unsafe for you to ingest. Allow the drops to linger in your mouth without swallowing.

✠ Take a brief moment to *feel* the spirit's potency working its way through your body, preparing you for the dream-work to come. Your hands or feet may start to feel warm. Depending on your skills of perception, you may feel a "wave" wash through you.

✠ Go to bed as you usually do, and do your best to forget the charm you have placed upon yourself. A watched pot never boils, as they say, so let it go, and let it be.

Feel no trepidation about experimenting with your own spirit flight process in order to find the approach that works best for you. When working with plant essences, spirit water, or even tinctures, one might add a few drops to a warm bath as well, which has the added benefit of relaxing the body for a deep sleep. One might also add a few drops to a cup of herbal tea with a gentle sedative effect, such as chamomile or passionflower. Just be mindful, as always, of your safety and of your own medical conditions.

Perhaps the greatest use of spirit flight is the achievement of visitation at the witch's sabbat, a gathering of the spirits of witches living and dead alongside the otherworldly beings with whom we share communion. Admission to the witch's sabbat cannot be granted by any living person, nor can it be achieved by mere "visualization." Entrance to this hidden place is granted as a blessing, and cannot be forced, though it is easier to return once one has been admitted the first time. It is an ecstasy held in audience with ancient spirits who are, in a way, the ancestors of our craft. It is occasionally stumbled upon by new witches during spirit flight before they realize what is happening, which can be frightening if one is not prepared.

Saying anything about the ecstasy of the sabbat is much like saying nothing at all. The experience of this communion, which is both an ethereal place and a state of being, can be quite different for witches depending on their culture and their gifts. This much I can say: it is impossible to be welcomed into this place if one is found unworthy in the eyes of certain Old Ones, spirits who are very ancient and widely feared for their mastery of our craft. If the prospect of approaching fearsome beings gives you pause, then there is no need to seek them out. Perhaps that experience is not for you—at least not yet. In time, as our gifts develop, we are often able to look on dark spirits with kinder eyes. After all, haven't we—witches and charmers all—been described as "fearsome" ourselves, especially by those who do not know us well?

Part Two:
Recipes

A Note of Caution

Herbs are not, in and of themselves, "gentle," "harmless," or "wholesome." Herbs are plants, and plants contain chemical compounds that have very real effects on the body when touched, inhaled, or ingested. Many modern medicines are derived from isolated chemical compounds found, at least originally, within plants. Be smart, and consult your doctor before working with any plant that may pose a risk to your health. Be careful of exposing loved ones, especially children, pets, or the elderly, to herbs that may not be safe for them.

For each of the following recipes, I've also provided an alternative formulation using spirit water, oil, or salts, which captures the magical potency of the plant in a given preparation without the need to touch or ingest any of the actual plant matter.

Even if you know for certain that a plant is safe for you to work with, you may wish to dilute its formula in order to avoid its side effects. A chamomile infusion, for example, might make you quite drowsy, when your goal was merely to experience the solar potencies of the plant spirit. Dilution allows us to lessen the medicinal effects of herbs. By adding a very small amount of the prepared infusion to a larger amount of the carrier substance (be it water, oil, or what have you), we can reduce (but not eliminate, mind you) its biochemical effects on the body.

Preparing Herbs

In most formulas, it is unwise to simply pull herbs from the ground and work with them without cleaning and drying first. Without this necessary step, we risk ingesting bits of soil or insects. Preparing herbs is also a pleasant way of honoring the material the plant has given us, showing it a bit of additional respect by cleaning and drying its body by hand.

Note: Not all plants are safe to handle and consume for all persons. If a plant poses any danger to you, consider using the formula for plant spirit water instead (pages 146-149), which does not require harvesting or even touching the plant. Spirit water may also be ideal for rare and vulnerable plants that you do not wish to harm. These formulas are adaptable to preparations of oil, unguent, salt, powder, or any other substance or base.

- All freshly gathered herbs should be washed thoroughly to remove any insects or bits of soil, then patted as dry as possible using a cloth. Take care with this step, as herbs that are hung to dry with moisture still on them run the risk of growing mold, rendering them unusable.
- If preparing a leaf or flower essence, or if steeping a hot infusion of the fresh herb, the plant is ready to be utilized after washing and drying by hand.
- If preparing an infused oil, salt, powder, balm, or any formula

requiring dry herb, the washed and hand-dried plant should be tied together into a bundle and hung to dry completely. Take care that the bundle is not too large; a great mass tied together will take far longer to dry and risk developing mold from trapped moisture in the process. Tie smaller bundles roughly the size of your wrist to speed the drying process.

✠ Hang these bundles in an area of your home that has good air circulation, warmth, and no direct sunlight, being sure that no children, pets, or guests will come into unwanted contact with them. Be warned that the herbs will "shed" a bit, dropping bits of plant matter as they shrink in the drying process. Any fallen plant matter should be discarded.

✠ Once the drying process is complete, the herbs should be ground, chopped, or lightly torn (if desired), then stored in an airtight jar to be used within 2 years.

Infusions

An infusion can be either hot or cold. The most common form of hot infusion is simply tea, in which dried or fresh herbs are steeped in hot water. Cold infusions usually involve fresh herbs left in cold water for a longer period of time. Infusions can be consecrated using the basic ritual outline found on pages 86-96. While the recipes provided here are fairly standard for infusions, be mindful that some herbs may require different ratios due to their unique qualities.

For a typical hot infusion (tea):
- Steep 3 tsp of fresh herb or 1 tsp of dried herb in one cup of boiled water for 5-8 minutes.
- A proper steep for potent magical purposes should be covered so as to lose as little steam as possible.
- The tea is then strained. It can be stored in the fridge for 1-2 days, if necessary.

For a typical cold infusion:
- Dried herbs are best. Place 1 tsp of dried, thoroughly broken herbs into a glass container, then add just enough water to dampen the herbs to prevent them from floating too much.
- Pour in one cup of cold, clean water, then store in a cold place for up to 12 hours.

✠ Take care with this preparation; since it has not been heated, any bacteria introduced can proliferate rapidly. The resulting infusion should be used quickly before it spoils.

Note: Not all herbs are safe for preparation as infusions. If a plant poses any danger to you, it may be safer to add three drops of the plant's spirit water (see pages 146-149) to hot water or to a prepared infusion that is safe for you to consume.

Essences

A flower or leaf essence is a magical plant medicine that contains almost no actual plant matter, but has instead been "imprinted" with the magical potency of the plant using water and sunlight. The flower essence formula most commonly used today was developed by Dr. Edward Bach. Not all herbal practitioners agree over how flower essences work, but for the witch's purposes, what matters most is that they replicate the properties of morning dew left on the flower, which has been used in folk magic for hundreds of years. Like all other herbal preparations, flower and leaf essences may be consecrated using the process on pages 86-96.

Leaf essences are a popular modern variation that allows us to work with the non-floral aspects of the plant in essence form. All essences require either sunlight or moonlight, so plan according to the weather. Though I have heard mention of practitioners experimenting with "root essences," I am skeptical of this formulation due to the introduction of soil and fungus to the vessel of water. Both flower and leaf essences are usually taken orally, but may also be added to bath water or used to consecrate clothing, jewelry, or any other objects.

✠ Fill a clear glass bowl with about two cups of fresh, cold water, preferably spring water, well water, or filtered water. Avoid using water sold in plastic bottles if you can.

✠ Carry this outside, and pick anywhere from 3-9 fresh, healthy flowers or leaves, depending on size, setting them upon the surface of the water to drift.

✠ Leave the bowl in either direct sunlight or moonlight for two hours in cold weather or one hour in hot weather. Consider using moonlight instead of sunlight for lunar herbs or those with nocturnal potencies.

✠ Once the allotted time is up, remove the plant matter with a twig or a wooden spoon, and filter the water through a fine cloth or coffee filter. The resulting fluid should be perfectly clear with no visible particles or coloration.

✠ Now, begin a series of dilutions:

- ❖ Mix this water with an equal part brandy. This results in the "mother essence," which is not consumed, but is used to prepare the "stock bottle."
- ❖ Add three drops of this mother essence to a new fluid ounce of equal parts water and brandy. This forms the "stock" essence. Again, this is not consumed, but is used to prepare our final formulation: the "dosage bottle."
- ❖ Finally, dilute again, adding three drops of this "stock" essence to a new glass dropper bottle containing one fluid ounce of equal parts water and brandy. This is the dosage bottle which can be used, taking three drops up to three times daily.

Note: Flower and leaf essences are usually regarded as safe for most people due to their thorough dilution, but there is still a small chance of ingesting microscopic particles of plant matter. When working with poisonous plants, it may be safer to use the spirit water formula (provided on pages 146-149), which may be used in place of the stock bottle essence to derive dosage bottles.

Tinctures

A tincture is an herbal preparation that extracts more of the plant's components into a smaller amount of fluid. This is accomplished by using alcohol and allowing the formula to sit for a longer period of time before filtering and straining. The resulting preparation has a very long shelf life of up to three years, depending on storage conditions. Tinctures can be consecrated to a magical purpose using the basic ritual outline on pages 86-96.

The dosage for tinctures is measured in drops or dropperfuls, and it is usually taken mixed with a small amount of water. It may also be applied to the surface of objects to imbue them with the plant's spiritual potencies. While the recipe provided here is fairly standard for tinctures, bear in mind that some herbs require an adjustment to the ratio of herb to spirit due to their unique properties.

- Before preparing a tincture, clean your hands and your tools well. You will need a bottle, a funnel, and a knife and cutting board if the herb is not already crushed.
- Fill a glass jar anywhere from 1/3 to 2/3 of the way full with the dried and crushed flowers and/or leaves, then fill with either vodka or brandy and seal thoroughly. It is important that whatever alcohol spirit you choose to use be at least 40% alcohol by volume.

✠ Allow this mixture to sit for one to three lunar cycles (about 3-9 weeks), depending on the desired strength. Check the alcohol level often during this time. It should be high enough to cover the plant matter. Shake the jar every so often to help move the herbs around in the alcohol and aid the extraction process a bit.

✠ After the allotted time has passed, filter and strain the mixture using fine cloth or coffee filters and store it in a dropper bottle for use.

✠ Store the tincture in a cool, dark place for up to three years. Some herbalists have claimed to make tinctures that last up to 10 years, but I prefer to be overly cautious. With tinctures more than six months old, inspect the liquid carefully for any mold or odd-looking growth. If it looks or smells different than when it was bottled, I recommend discarding it.

Note: Not all herbs are safe for use in tinctures. If an herb is unsafe for you to ingest, consider following the formula for plant spirit water instead (pages 146-149), substituting brandy or vodka for water in the smaller vessel.

Vinegars

Vinegar was the household cleaning agent of choice in previous ages, and it is gentle enough to use regularly when diluted with water, even on antique wood floors and furniture. Due to its history of use, a vinegar preparation may be ideal for the magical "washing" of one's home or property. If the herbs used are safe to ingest, an herbal vinegar may also be used in salad dressings or various recipes. Do mind the smell, of course, which can be quite distracting if you are hosting guests later that day after cleaning with vinegar. Vinegars may be consecrated using the ritual process on pages 86-96.

- Place a small amount of dried herb into a well-cleaned glass jar or bottle, then fill the remainder of the way with white vinegar. A good starting ratio would be one tbsp of dried herb to one cup of vinegar, though one can always play with the measurements in order to produce a weaker or stronger result.
- Be wary of exposing the vinegar to metal, as the two substances will react. Consider using a vessel with a cork or non-metal stopper to avoid this problem.
- Allow the mixture to sit for one lunar cycle (roughly three weeks), then filter and strain using fine cloth or coffee filters, then bottle for storage.
- Use the vinegar within six months for best results—or consider

storing in a refrigerator to preserve it longer.

✠ To create a gentle cleaning solution for floors and surfaces, dilute one part vinegar in nine parts water. Be mindful that the herbs chosen for the vinegar are safe for pets, children, and guests; what is safe for oneself is not always safe for others.

Note: Not all herbs are safe to use in vinegars. If an herb is unsafe for you, consider using the plant spirit water formula instead (pages 146-149), substituting vinegar in the smaller vessel.

Oils

Infused oils are quite the versatile preparation in magical herbalism. Because the oil is imbued with the spiritual potencies of the plant, it can be used to anoint the forehead or pulse points, to consecrate objects, or even to bless doorways. An infused oil is also the basic ingredient needed in order to craft an ointment, unguent, or balm. Infused oils can be consecrated using the basic ritual outline on pages 86-96.

There are two simple methods for producing an herb-infused oil, one being fast and the other slow.

If using the slow method:
- Fill a very clean glass jar ¾ of the way with the crushed herb, then add enough oil to nearly fill the vessel. Both extra virgin olive oil and sweet almond oil will yield good results, but some prefer sunflower oil.
- Seal the vessel, and place it in a warm windowsill where the sun can heat the mixture gently over time.
- Allow it to sit for one to three lunar cycles (about 3-9 weeks), depending on the desired strength. Give the jar a good shake every now and then to aid the process.
- The infused oil must then be filtered and strained thoroughly using cheesecloth or some other fine cloth, removing all plant

matter.

✣ If you wish to preserve your infused oil for a long shelf life, consider adding vitamin E or using the oil to prepare an ointment, salve, or balm, which is naturally stabilized and preserved by the inclusion of beeswax.

If using the fast method:

✣ Preheat your oven to just under 200 degrees Fahrenheit. (The ideal temperature for individual ovens may vary; the point is to heat the herbs gently, but not fry them in the oil.)

✣ Place the herb and oil mixture (with the same ratios as the slow method) into an open glass jar, and set this jar in a water bath in a larger baking dish.

✣ Allow the oil to infuse in the oven for at least four hours, then remove and **allow to cool before proceeding**.

✣ The infused oil must then be filtered by using cheesecloth or some other fine cloth to remove all plant matter.

✣ If you wish to preserve your infused oil for a long shelf life, consider adding vitamin E oil or using the oil to prepare an ointment, salve, or balm, which is naturally stabilized and preserved by the inclusion of beeswax.

Note: Not all herbs are safe to use in oils. If an herb is unsafe for you to use topically, consider using the plant spirit water formula instead (pages 146-149), substituting sweet almond oil or virgin olive oil in the smaller vessel.

Ointments, Salves, and Balms

The witch's ointment, made famous in the folklore of "flying ointments" and "witch's grease," is a magical staple for very practical reasons. The beeswax that is mixed with the infused oil preserves it for a longer shelf life, and its thickness circumvents the messiness of dripping. Because an unguent does not absorb into the skin as quickly as an oil, one is, in effect, "wearing" the plant as a kind of external layer, which can have many magical meanings. The rubbing and massaging of one's own (or another person's) skin with the slippery mixture also has a very specific ritual effect that can be quite hypnotic and stimulating. All unguents can be consecrated using the ritual formula on pages 86-96.

Ointments, salves, and balms are all made from infused oils and beeswax; it is only the ratio of oil to wax that differentiates these preparations.

- For an ointment, use five parts infused oil to one part beeswax.
- For a salve, use four parts infused oil to one part beeswax.
- For a balm, use three parts infused oil to one part beeswax.

An ointment is quite soft and viscous, while a salve is a bit firmer. A balm is quite firm. Looser preparations will have a shorter shelf-life than firmer ones since it is the beeswax that acts as a preservative.

The process for crafting all three preparations is as follows:

- ✠ Pour the infused oil along with the desired amount of beeswax in a ceramic or glass vessel without a lid, preferably one with a pour spout on its lip. Consider using beeswax shavings, pellets, or otherwise broken bits since these will melt a bit faster.
- ✠ Place the vessel containing the oil and wax on a large tray for stability, and place in an oven set to just under 200 degrees Fahrenheit.
- ✠ Watch carefully, and remove the tray as soon as the wax is completely melted, then stir the vessel with a twig or toothpick to completely mix the wax and oil together.
- ✠ Using an oven mitt, and being careful to avoid burns, pour the hot unguent into your container of choice, and allow it to cool completely.

In my experience, a balm may last four years or more, while an ointment may only last for two years. Use your best judgment (and sense of smell) to determine when an unguent has gone bad.

Note: While unguents made from baneful plants have long been crafted by knowledgeable and experienced hands, there is always an element of risk involved in this process. Instead, I recommend using the spirit water formula (pages 146-149) for plants that may be harmful to you, substituting oil in the smaller vessel, and utilizing this oil as the basis for the unguent.

Powders

The witch's powder usually consists quite simply of herbs that have been ground very finely using a mortar and pestle. Magical powders may be sprinkled on the lines of one's property or on places where the intended magical target may tread, rendering their desired effect. They may also be "blown" either directly onto property or at a great distance, sent in the direction of the magical target, using the wind as a vehicle to reach their destination. Powders should be consecrated using a ritual, possibly the suggested ritual outline on pages 86-96.

Do not be surprised if it takes time and muscle to render a powder using this ancient method. The task of grinding herbs, rather than being seen as a chore, can become a kind of rhythmic meditation. Many of the Scottish folk songs that have survived to this day are actually songs for work—the rhythms of which would have accompanied repetitive tasks. Consider finding your own song or incantation for tasks like this one.

Note: Because powders become airborne quite easily, this formulation is best reserved for plants that are safe to consume. Even if using safe herbs, the powder should not be inhaled. If working with a baneful plant, consider instead using the plant spirit water formula on pages 146-149, substituting flour, cornmeal, or some other safe powder in the smaller vessel.

Salts

Magical salts have been used throughout the ages in purification and in the creation of sanctified water. This is one of many hallmarks of witchcraft that have come to us from the trappings of paganism-infused Catholicism, which flavored the folk magic of the early modern period. We see the use of blessed salt in many famous grimoires, including the *Clavicula Salomonis*. Witches can tailor the formulation of blessed salts using the plants of our choice in order to create a salt that is unique, dedicated to a specific form of blessing, cleansing, or guarding. A crafted herbal salt can be consecrated using the ritual process found on pages 86-96.

The simplest way to craft herb-infused salts is by applying a small amount of the herb's prepared tincture (see pages 123-124) to a vessel of dry salt, allowing the alcohol to evaporate, then stirring the salt thoroughly to break up any clumps.

Others prefer the inclusion of the raw herb in their salts, which can be accomplished by mixing a small amount of the herb in powdered form into the vessel of salt. If using this method, consider selecting a salt with a fineness or coarseness matching the prepared powder so that the two do not separate too much.

The prepared salt may be laid on a boundary line as a protective charm, sprinkled on one's property, added to baths, or dissolved in water (a mere pinch will do) to prepare blessed water. Salts do not expire and may be kept for many years so long as they remain dry.

Note: If a particular herb is not skin-safe for you, consider using the plant spirit water formula on pages 146-149 instead, substituting fresh salt in the smaller vessel. Powders can become airborne quite easily, so I recommend using caution and avoiding creating powders from herbs that may pose harm.

Incense

The use of magical fumigation has for centuries been associated with the calling of spirits. An incense crafted with one's own hands is an ideal spirit offering, not only to familiars and guides, but to spirits of the land around us, the dead, our ancestors, and any deities or saints with which one chooses to work in one's craft. Fumigations of any kind may be consecrated using the basic ritual outline on pages 86-96.

Incense also "bathes" us in the fluid, air-born, spiritual substance of the plant that is burned. An object held within this smoke can be consecrated to a specific purpose. A room filled with incense can be used to invite or expel a particular influence.

The simplest form of incense is dried and loose herb. The leaves or flowers of one or more plants, once thoroughly dried, may be sprinkled over a lit charcoal (in a safe vessel, mind you) to produce smoke. This is probably the oldest form of fumigation in existence, and it remains popular today due to its simplicity.

One may also dry a given herb in bundles, sometimes called "smudge sticks," though this name is more properly applied to Native American spiritual practices. To dry herbs in bundles, one may tie them very tightly while still fresh using a thread or fiber that is safe to burn, or simply braid them together, tying the ends. The benefit of preparing bundles is that one may burn the herb while holding it and wafting its smoke in a particular direction, which gives us greater control than simply burning the herb in a vessel.

While there are methods for preparing incense cones and sticks oneself, I find these recipes very fussy and inconvenient, and all of them depend on purchased ingredients that must be shipped from far away. If you wish to craft an incense that is more convenient than a bundle or loose blend, consider grinding the herb thoroughly, then using a small amount of honey and water to roll the mixture into "pellets" that may be dropped onto burning charcoal. These should be no larger than blueberries in order to ensure even burning, and they must be allowed to dry thoroughly in a warm place before using.

An even simpler approach can be found by applying a prepared tincture of a given herb to purchased incense cones or sticks. Just be quite careful to allow the alcohol to **completely evaporate** before lighting, which may take quite a while depending on how thoroughly the tincture is applied. Do not light until the incense is bone-dry and all risk of flammability from the alcohol has passed. Remember that the vapor released from evaporating alcohol can sometimes be flammable as well, so the treated incense should be left to dry in the open air to avoid the risk of trapped fumes.

Note: Many plants are unsafe to burn, producing smoke that can harm the body. If an herb is unsafe for you to use as incense, consider using the plant spirit water formula on pages 146-149 instead, adding a drop of the plant's prepared spirit water to a purchased incense cone, and allowing it to dry completely before burning. Even if an herb is safe for you to burn, always do so in a well-ventilated area.

Inks

Plant-based inks are surprisingly simple to concoct, and they lend themselves well to sigils, pacts, and sacred artistry. By experimenting with different plants from the land around us, we can arrive at colors that are complex and surprising in ways that store-bought inks can never quite achieve. All inks, like all other herbal formulations, can be consecrated using the process on pages 86-96.

Keep in mind that the final color is not necessarily predictable by the color of the plant; dandelion flowers will result in a very light green, and purple deadnettle flowers will result in a near-black. Though I have not experimented with browned and reddened leaves in the fall, some natural ink-makers tout the vibrance of the colors achieved this way.

- Begin with 4 cups of lightly packed fresh leaves and/or flowers of the selected plant.
- Bring the herbs to boil in a covered pot with 2 cups of water, 2 tbsp of vinegar, and a pinch of salt.
- Lower the heat, and simmer for 15 minutes, covered.
- Remove the pot from the heat and allow to cool. Strain the plant matter from the liquid using cheesecloth or coffee filters.
- Return this strained liquid to a clean pot and bring to a boil again. Boil this liquid to reduce its volume until you achieve

the concentration you desire. The more the liquid is reduced, the darker the final ink will be.

✣ Don't be afraid to take your time in achieving the right concentration. One can always allow the liquid to cool, then test it on a bit of paper. If it isn't dark enough, return the liquid to the pot, and reduce further.

✣ Some plants will yield an ink that is quite viscous and may work better with a fine brush or a feather quill than with modern fountain pens, which have very narrow metal grooves designed for commercial inks.

Note: Crafting herbal inks requires considerable boiling, and the steam from some plants may cause harmful reactions in certain individuals. If a plant isn't safe for you, consider using the plant spirit water formula on pages 146-149 instead and adding one drop of prepared spirit water to a purchased bottle of ink.

Talismans

Although the herbal talisman may take countless forms in modern witchcraft, the most common forms are simple herb talisman, the sachet, and the witch's bottle. The "plant-veiled stone," though less popular today, once went by many names, including the serpent stone or root stone. None of these creations are consumed internally or applied externally, but instead rely on the folk-magical principle of contagion to administer their potency via proximity to the person who carries them or the space within which they are placed. Like all other herbal formulations, talismans can be consecrated following the basic ritual outline on pages 86-96.

The simple herb talisman is the least fussy of these, often consisting of a nut or seed carried in the pocket, a dried leaf kept in the sole of the shoe, a flower pinned on the inside or outside of one's clothing, or a dried root kept in a particular location. Magical use is ingrained in the history of the bouquet, the corsage, and the boutonniere, and as we see in the lore of many plants, the most common form of plant talisman is often simply a sprig tucked in a pocket or a flower set in a vase in the home.

The plant-veiled stone is a worthy alternative for a talisman composed of the plant itself. This is often called a *serpent stone* in old herbal lore, but this is a bit confusing, since holed stones are also sometimes referred to as serpent stones. A plant's stone was once said to be found under or around many herbs (often heather or plantain) and to bear strong magical properties. Simply allow your intuition to help you locate a small stone near the plant. *This is a wise charm if a particular plant is unsafe for you to touch and work with.*

The herbal sachet usually consists of a small amount of dried herb—be it leaves, flowers, or roots—sewn inside a piece of cloth or paper. It is often embroidered or painted with symbols representing the magical goal. Though selecting the appropriate plant is the most obvious choice to be made here, there are many other decisions involved in the sachet's construction, and each of them should be deliberate and related to the purpose of the working:

- What color paper or fabric best represents the purpose of the sachet? The interpretation of color can vary greatly by one's culture, but in my own practice, red often represents vigor, energy, and vitality, while white represents cleansing, beginnings, and clarity. Gray, in my craft, represents transformation and shifting energy, while black represents stasis, stillness, and endurance.
- What shape best represents the goal of the sachet? A square, for example, is strong, but immobile, like a weighty stone. It does not roll, but stays. A triangle points upward or downward, suggesting growth or change in one direction or another. A circle is whole and complete, suggesting satisfaction and wellness.

✠ What symbols or embellishments best represent the goal? The decoration of the sachet can be as ornate or simple as one desires, involving the use of Norse bind-runes, ogham staves, the letters of the Theban alphabet, sigils derived from spirit communication, or even simple pictorial illustrations. As with most things, simplicity offers the best path for beginners: a cross can represent protection and stability; an eye can represent knowledge and perception; corn or wheat can represent prosperity, etc.

✠ *Note: If an herb is unsafe for you, it is always a viable alternative to simply craft the sachet using a safer filling material, then consecrate it by applying a few drops of plant spirit water or oil (pages 146-149).*

The witch's bottle may be carried on the person like a sachet, but more often, it is placed in a particular room within a dwelling or work space. It may also be buried on one's property. The herbs selected for the bottle should represent different aspects of the need at hand, much like words strung together to form a sentence. Although exceedingly popular among modern witches today, the witch's bottle is, in fact, an old and well-established tradition of folk-magical practice. Archaeologists have unearthed witch's bottles dating back to ancient Greece, not to mention the very famous witch's bottles found all over the British Isles dating to the 1500s and before.

Witch's bottles are usually less ornately adorned, but other objects are often sealed along with the herbs, including the target's hair or fingernails—or sometimes a bit of paper with symbols or words representing the magical goal. A very punishing, malefic witch's bottle may include rusted nails and urine—with the intention of inflicting harm upon the target. Likewise, the inclusion of sweet-smelling flowers, coins, and other pleasantries may be used to confer blessings.

Note: If handling the material of a particular herb is unsafe for you, it is always acceptable to include a bit of soil or stone gathered near a plant as a replacement for the plant itself. Again, be sure not to dig too deep nor too close to the plant so as to avoid its roots.

Dollies and Roots

Much like the spirit vessel, the corn dolly or herb dolly functions as a portable home for the spirit of a plant, which may be brought indoors and hung on the wall or given a respectful spot on an altar or bookshelf. In previous ages, observance of this superstition was a way of bringing the spirit of a harvest indoors during the cold winter months so that it may return the following year. Today, it may be used to offer a second spiritual home to a plant so that their magical potency may be "brought in" to affect a particular outcome, or simply out of love for the plant spirit itself. Dollies may be consecrated using the ritual outline found on pages 86-96.

The simplest dollies are crafted by braiding the leaves or stems of the plant itself, then tying both ends in either a strand or a connected loop, but there has always been a great deal of variation in their make. Consider experimenting with braiding or knotting the stems or long leaves of a particular plant in order to arrive at a design that speaks to you.

If the plant produces fruit or berries, it may be preferable to collect these when ripe and dry them. Small berries may be strung with a needle and thread, then hung in a warm spot to dry. Fruits may be sliced, then strung likewise into garlands. In Scottish folk magic, the dried berries of the rowan tree are sometimes used, while in Appalachian folk magic, beans, peppers, and sometimes other plants are dried in garlands in a similar way.

The root of a plant, which is its underworldly body concealed in the dark below us, can be exhumed and dried as a kind of magical relic, capable of housing the spirit like any dolly, but in a way that emphasizes the plant's unseen, darker, or more chthonic properties. The winding, hairy structure of a plant's root adapts to stones or neighboring root systems in its soil, making each plant's root a unique structure indicative of a distinct personality. In this way, a dried root is also a way of fondly remembering a plant that has reached the end of its life cycle (the other important way being to gather its seeds for future sowing).

Note: Not all plants are safe to hang in the home, since they will "shed" while drying out and may be picked up by children or pets. A worthy substitute would be a braided bit of common wheat, corn husks, or recycled fabric treated with a few drops of plant spirit water (recipe on pages 146-149).

Plant Spirit Water

(& Plant Spirit Oils, Powders, Vinegars, Salts, etc.)

Plant spirit preparations are a safer way of working with baneful or poisonous plants to prepare any formula to be used internally or externally. While flower essences and other diluted preparations of baneful herbs can be relatively safe when made by experienced hands, even a simple mistake in their preparation can result in lethal danger. I recommend preparing plant spirit water instead if you have any doubts about your safety. This method is grounded in the principle of magical transference via contagion and is related to the old folklore of pacts or exchanges with spirits. Plant spirit water may be consecrated using the basic ritual process outlined on pages 86-96.

This preparation involves an exchange of offerings: water given for the nourishment of the plant, and water taken in order to apply the plant spirit's potency in herbal preparations. Though this specific charm is my own modern adaptation, it is derived from two distinct folkloric traditions. It is partly adapted from old lustration charms involving palmfuls of water used to bless and anoint, several of which survive in texts such as the *Carmina Gadelica*. It is also adapted from old pact-making superstitions in which something is promised to the plant spirit in exchange for a favor of some kind, a pattern of charm-work that appears in many places, including the folklore of the elder tree.

✠ To begin, prepare a small, sealed vessel of spring water or filtered water. This small bottle will house your spirit water, so consider choosing something glass or ceramic rather than plastic.

✠ You will also need a larger vessel for pouring—perhaps a pitcher or glass jar. This should also be filled with clean, fresh, cold water.

✠ Sitting near the plant itself, place the sealed bottle of water on the ground near the plant's base—where its roots are likely to be. Holding one cupped hand over the bottle, pour the fresh water so that it flows into your palm, spilling out from your hand and pouring over the sealed bottle and into the soil at the plant's base.

✠ You can use any words you choose to make clear the exchange, but you might consider the following:

> *For thy growth and for thy bounty,*
> *a portion from me to thee.*
> *and in return for this fair share,*
> *a portion from thee to me.*

✠ Once the water has all been poured and absorbed into the soil, the offering has been made. Watch and listen carefully for signs that the plant has reciprocated the offering; you may experience a feeling or simply notice a change in the sounds of birds or weather around you. In any case, the vessel of sealed water should "feel" different now, being imbued with the plant spirit's potency.

✟ When the feeling is right, collect the now blessed vessel of plant spirit water from the ground.

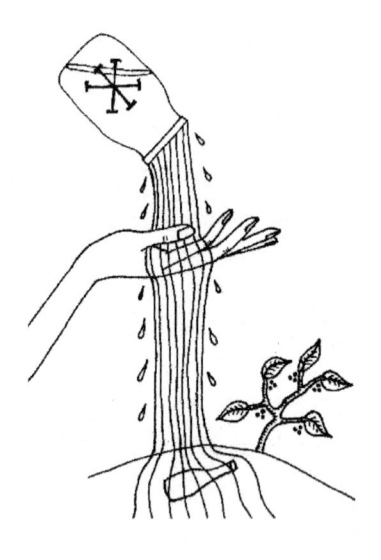

This basic formula can be adapted in a great variety of ways as a legitimate substitute for the actual plant matter of herbs:

✟ For an infusion substitute, add three drops of plant spirit water to a cup of hot water or to a prepared infusion of another herb that is safe for you to consume.

✟ For a flower essence substitute, add three drops of plant spirit water to one fluid ounce composed of 50% brandy and 50% clean water.

✠ For a tincture substitute, add one drop of plant spirit water to a small amount of spirit (vodka or brandy, usually).

✠ For an incense substitute, place one drop of plant spirit water on a purchased incense cone, and allow to dry completely in a warm place.

✠ For an ink substitute, add one drop of plant spirit water to a small bottle of store-bought ink.

✠ For a powder substitute, follow the plant spirit water formula, substituting flour, cornmeal, or some other powder that is safe for you in the small sealed vessel.

✠ For an infused oil substitute, follow the plant spirit water formula, substituting sweet almond oil or virgin olive oil in the small sealed vessel.

✠ For an infused salt substitute, follow the plant spirit water formula, substituting salt in the small sealed vessel.

✠ For an infused vinegar substitute, follow the plant spirit water formula, substituting vinegar in the small sealed vessel.

✠ For a dried herb talisman substitute, apply three drops of plant spirit water onto a stone, seashell, or some other natural object, and allow to dry.

✠ For a sachet substitute, prepare the sachet with a safe filling material, then apply three drops of plant spirit water to the surface, and allow to dry.

Part Three:
Common Flora

Plant Lore Profiles

The following section of this guide is made up of individual profiles on common plants, including some of their folklore, their history of use, and some of my own observations on the magical signatures I read in them. Allow yourself, dear reader, to form your own relationships with these plants and others. Approach these profiles as examples for your own work. Make use of what helps you along your own path, but bear in mind that the same plant can reveal different aspects to different practitioners, for what we perceive and what we need are often related to our cultural background and to our own individual proclivities as charmers. Perceiving an aspect of an ancient spirit that is not described in this book or others is not a sign of failure; it might very well be a sign of success in the development of your own craft. When we permit ourselves to make the spiritual encounter without preconceived notions, we are often surprised by what we find.

Do note that this section includes information on the folklore of plants that are edible and medicinal as well as plants that are poisonous and potentially lethal. Because the varieties of a given plant may differ considerably, and because the medical conditions and sensitivities of the human body can vary even more so, it is the sole responsibility of the practitioner—in coordination a trusted physician—to determine which plants are safe for them to touch or consume. Any plant you choose to work with via touch or ingestion is a risk you take on your own.

I recommend consulting a good foraging guide for an introduction on identifying safe plants, but I also recommend speaking with your doctor, especially if you are pregnant, have allergies, or have any underlying medical conditions that may affect your relationship with a given plant. Remember that many plants have dangerous look-alikes; it is wise to consult with an expert in order to be certain of the species of a plant in your area. Remember, too, that even safe plants may be exposed to harmful contaminants if they grow by roadsides or other human structures where they are exposed to waste or pollution.

Due to the popularity of viral social media videos on foraging, there exists a great deal of confusion about what "edibility" means. Just because a plant is edible does not mean that it tastes good, nor does it mean that the plant has no biochemical effect on the body when consumed. Many plants listed as edible in foraging guides are quite unpleasant to taste, and some of them have medicinal actions that may or may not be desirable to the practitioner. The fact that they are edible simply means the body can digest them—with or without some unpleasantness in the process.

Thankfully, and I cannot stress this enough, *it is not necessary to touch a plant in order to work with it magically.* If you have any doubts at all about the safety of a plant, consider using the plant spirit water formulas on pages 146-149 in order to access the plant's magical potencies without exposing yourself to its toxins. These formulas are also preferable for rare plants or in places where it is illegal to pick or harm local flora.

As you work with these and other plants, you may wish to gather their seeds in order to sow intentionally for the following year of growth. Be mindful of which species in your area are local and which are invasive. Though all plants have their magical strengths, introducing some species in an area where they can propagate unchecked can have negative impacts on local ecosystems. Indigenous plants often have not evolved to compete alongside aggressive invaders, and we should be careful to protect them when we can so that they, too, can thrive.

… 156 Roger J. Horne …

Agrimony

(Agrimonia Eupatoria, Agrimonia Rostellata,
and related species)

Folk names: Common Agrimony, Woodland Agrimony, Church's Steeples, Sticklewort, Cockeburr, Philanthropos, Grooveburr, Liverwort, Money-in-Both-Pockets, Rat's Tail, Sweetheart, Fairy's Wand, Eupatorium

Regions: Common in most regions that experience freezing winters, sometimes in differing varieties

Suggested Magical Uses: To Bless Friends and Loved Ones; To Defend Against Enemies and Wicked Spirits; To Bring Vitality and Strength

Agrimony is one of many ancient plants known for clinging seeds, which are frequently found stuck in one's clothing after strolling through a field. Its long and phallic stalks were boiled with milk by the Anglo-Saxons in order to treat erectile dysfunction. Agrimony's folk name *philanthropos* is reportedly related to its barbed seeds clinging to passersby (etymologically, *philanthropy* means "man-loving"). It is often said to represent thankfulness and gratitude in the Victorian language of flowers.

Most famously, though, agrimony is associated with protection and healing. In medieval times, it was said in the British Isles to cause a deep and pleasant sleep when laid under a person's head. It was recommended in ancient times as an antidote to the venom of serpents. In fact, its folk name *eupatorium* is reported to come from King Mithridates Eupator of Pontus, who famously used agrimony as an antidote when political enemies attempted to poison him. Common agrimony was, in classical times, celebrated as one of the "all-healing" herbs, recommended for all manner of woes. In Austria, it was said that agrimony could afford the user the ability to perceive dark spirits, especially the spirits of malefic witches.

Like many plants adored since ancient times, agrimony can be said to possess a complex mixture of potencies. In its phallic form and protective powers, it bears a martial nature, but it is also venereal in its clinging seeds and attractive, golden blooms, on which gather all manner of butterflies and moths. Its tall, prolific seed-head is emblematic of Jupiter's qualities of fruitfulness and prosperity, and its legendary healing powers speak to a solar potency. Agrimony is perhaps most well-suited, though, to the manipulation of virility and vitality, to render the enemy's attempts at harm impotent, and to strengthen the potency of one's own workings. It also has great potential for all manner of blessings bestowed upon friends and loved ones, especially to do with health and prosperity.

Archangel

(Lamium Purpureum)

Folk names: *Dead Nettle, Purple Dead Nettle, Red Dead Nettle, Purple Archangel, St. Mary's Hand*
Regions: Common in most regions that experience freezing winters
Suggested Magical Uses: To Bring Comfort, To Bring Joy in the Midst of Sadness, To Ease Loneliness

Red or purple dead nettle, also called *archangel*, is a springtime plant, often one of the first to flower when warmth returns after winter, its bright purple flowerheads being one of the first sources of sustenance for honeybees. It often grows in great throngs near disturbed earth, and often in partially shaded locations. Its heart-shaped leaves fade from a bright green to a deep purple hue near the tip of each stalk, erupting in very small, trumpet-like purple flowers. Although technically a mint, its odor is distinct unto itself, being faintly musky when the plant is bruised or picked. The name *dead nettle* has long been used to differentiate the plant from stinging nettles. There exist a white and a yellow variety (called *white* and *yellow* dead nettle, respectively), and though these are of a very similar nature, they tend to bloom much later.

In France, the plant has been called *St. Mary's Hand*. This, along with the name *archangel*, denote the red dead nettle's association with the festivals of the Annunciation, which take place in late March. We can view archangel's association with comfort and joy in the midst of upheaval as related to both its early spring bloom, sometimes even coinciding with frost, and its merging with Christian mythology pertaining to the archangel's message to Mary, signifying a kind of hope for the future. One need not be Christian to notice the friendly and gentle nature of this plant for oneself, though. It emerges as an ally at a time of the year when we are still shaking off the cold and dark, and it is reported to have been boiled and eaten historically as a spring green. (Personally, I find the smell of boiled dead nettle quite unpleasant.)

Interestingly, archangel's love of shade and musky scent reveal a somewhat saturnine nature in its composition, though far gentler of course than many other saturnine plants, which can sometimes be poisonous. As a plant spirit, I find that archangel peers into the dark in order to set a candle within it, to rescue us from our various winters of the soul. Its heart-shaped leaves and attractiveness to bees speaks to a venereal nature as well, though it is more nurturing here than romantic, in my opinion. Though often overlooked as a magical plant, archangel should be strongly considered in charm-work aimed at alleviating depression, loneliness, and weariness from a long difficulty, for its nature is to provide much-needed comfort in these times.

Bitter Dock

(Rumex Obtusifolius)

Folk names: Broadleaf Dock; Broad-Leaved Dock; Bluntleaf Dock; Butter Dock; Sour Dock
Regions: Common in most regions that experience freezing winters, as well as some tropical regions
Suggested Magical Uses: To Chase Away Strife or Suffering; To Hold Together Bonds of Love and Family; To Preserve What Is Cherished Against Adversity

One of many "docks" that can look quite similar, the bitter dock is one of the most well-distributed plants in the world, having a footprint in nearly every region. Historically, it has a long use in folk medicine, especially as a topical treatment for skin irritation. It is often used by folk herbalists as a remedy for the irritating effects of stinging nettle. That bitter dock is said to frequently grow alongside its stinging cousin is a form of old folk wisdom: that the poison and the cure are not enemies, but sisters, much like jewelweed and poison ivy in North America, which are also said to grow near one another.

In Cornwall, the leaves of bitter dock were at one time used frequently as part of a healing charm which called on "three angels out of the East" in order to soothe a burn or inflammation of the skin. A related iteration of this charm is to this day known in the Appalachian region of North America, one version of which is preserved as follows:

> *There came three angels out of the East.*
> *One brought fire.*
> *Two brought frost.*
> *Out, fire. In, frost.*
> *So help you now*
> *in the name of [the trinity, our lord, etc.]*

In some parts of the British Isles, there exists a simpler and less biblical version of the same charm. This iteration of the "out, in" charm draws more closely on the relationship between the bitter dock and the stinging nettle:

> *Out, Nettle. In, Dock.*
> *Dock shall have a new smock.*

Another version found in England is even simpler yet:

> *Dock, in. Nettle, out.*
> *Dock rub Nettle out.*

The folk name *butter dock* is sometimes said to be derived from the leaves being used to wrap fresh butter in previous eras. In northern Europe, the plant was reportedly used in a kind of love charm, which involved wrapping two ripe but unopened blossoms together (representing two lovers to be joined) using a long leaf of bitter dock. If the blooms did not open (or some other ill omen occurred during the process), it was said that the two were ill-suited. Some old herbals have suggested that the bitter dock held the connotation of patience in ancient Greece and Rome, but this is possibly a confusion with *rumex patienta*, a related but different species.

The abundance of reddish-brown seeds that explode from the stalks of the bitter dock reveal a clear jovial nature, while its suitability for the healing arts speaks to a certain solar potency as well. We can view the use of this plant in love charms as a different variety than typical venereal charms, this one being performed not by a lover themselves but by a third party watching carefully for signs of an ill-suited match. This sort of endeavor has more to do with Jupiter than Venus, as it relates to fitness and compatibility in the eyes of family and community more than desire and infatuation.

Bittersweet Nightshade
(Solanum Dulcamara)

Folk names: *Bitter Nightshade, Woody Nightshade, Enchanter's Nightshade, Dulcamara, Amara Dulcis, Felonwood, Felonwort, Scarlet Berry, Violet Bloom, Blue Bindweed, Climbing Nightshade, Snakeberry, Poisonberry*
Regions: Common in most of Europe and parts of North America
Suggested Magical Uses: To Bring Protection; To Halt the Enemy's Efforts; To Strike Fear Into the Enemy; To Achieve Visions or Dreams; To Open Gates Between Worlds

The bittersweet nightshade, which is related to black nightshade but very different in appearance, was both feared and adored in the ancient world, for it was at one time valued as an herb inducing sleep and relieving pain, but has always been considered at least somewhat poisonous. Cases of poisoning with bittersweet are less common than other nightshades due to its unpleasant taste, but the solanine toxin found within this plant is not to be trifled with, bringing at the very least a miserable sickness—if not outright death. Its occasional names *felonwood* and *felonwort* are not related to criminal activity, but to an infection caused by the herpes simplex virus that was at one time called *felon* or *whitlow*, a condition for which solanum dulcamara was, hundreds of years ago, considered effective.

In the British Isles, bittersweet was at one time hung on livestock to deter witches and faeries from cursing them. It has been used as a protective amulet in previous centuries for the same purpose. As a nightshade, though, this plant is also associated with the workings of witches. This paradox is similar in nature to that of the rowan tree, which is either beloved or feared by witches, depending on the lore at hand. We should view these little moments of irony as related to the divergence of "white witches" (cunning folk and magical practitioners who wished to be seen in a positive light) from "black witches" (hags, monsters, and other folkloric nasties, who often practiced arts known and used by the former type, even if they preferred not to be associated with "black witchcraft" categorically).

One tale associated with bittersweet nightshade is related to MacBeth (the historic figure, not the Shakesperean character). This nightshade was said to be used to poison the army of Sweno, King of Norway, as he attempted to negotiate the surrender of Duncan of Scotland. Once the poison had set in, the men became weakened and fell into a deep sleep, after which, they were easily slaughtered by MacBeth.

When considering the three "sister" nightshades of belladonna, black nightshade, and bittersweet together, we can consider bittersweet the gentlest of the three, capable of halting the efforts of the enemy and magically arresting their success against us.

Whereas black nightshade is useful in cursing, and belladonna even more so, bittersweet brings protection and a stern warning to the enemy, striking fear without the intense suffering of a more malefic curse. Like its saturnine sisters, it is also potent in arts related to otherworldly traveling, the opening of gates, and the achievement of visionary states.

Black Nightshade

(Solanum Nigrum, Solanum Ptychanthum)

Folk names: *Garden Nightshade, Poisonberry, Common Nightshade, Inkberry, Hound's Berry, Glossy Nightshade, Small-Flowered Nightshade, Petty Morel*

Regions: Common in most regions that experience freezing winters, as well as some tropical regions

Suggested Magical Uses: To Make Pacts with Spirits; To Curse the Enemy; To Open Gates Between Worlds

Black nightshade is sometimes confusingly referred to as "deadly nightshade" in older herbals due to its fruit, which does somewhat resemble the berries of the belladonna plant. Its flowers are quite distinct, though, being small and very delicate blooms of white and yellow. The American variety (*solanum ptychanthum*) has glossy berries, while the berries of the *solanum nigrum* are typically more matte in appearance. Most varieties of black nightshade contain levels of the toxin solanine that are dangerous to the body, resulting in gastrointestinal pain, fever, diarrhea, vomiting, confusion, heart failure, and death, though less frequently than with its cousin, deadly nightshade.

We can view black nightshade, which is found growing frequently in gardens and backyards, as a more common cousin of belladonna or deadly nightshade, possessing many of its qualities of alluring, dangerous beauty, but with a slightly less baneful potency to its poisonous personality. It serves as a worthy substitute for deadly nightshade in many charms.

Its name *inkberry* stems from the very dark stain left when an insect or bird breaks open its fruit, which is filled with black juice. For this reason, black nightshade is sometimes used in charm-work to do with pacts, or agreements forged between the practitioner and certain spirits, conferring certain blessings or gifts in exchange for negotiated offerings made by the witch.

Like its cousin belladonna, black nightshade has a very strong saturnine potency and lends itself well to otherworldly journeying and the opening of gates between worlds, including the achievement of the ecstasies of the witch's sabbat, which is viewed in folk and traditional witchcraft as an ecstatic state achieved by the practitioner, a blissful communion with the spirits of the dead, the land, and the otherworld for a time. This is sometimes achieved through dreamwork, but more often by using repetitive chants and motions that induce an altered state of consciousness.

Interestingly, black nightshade was reportedly used in ancient times as an herbal medicine under the name *petty morel*. It was apparently favored for its ability to expel fluid from the body via sweating and was also used to induce sleep or relieve pain. Even in ancient times, though, it was considered a dangerous remedy, and we can probably attribute any healing properties recorded in historical materia medica to the fact that a great many varieties of black nightshade exist, many almost indistinguishable, meaning the patient could be exposed to a cure or to a poison in this gamble. Such risks might have been worth the possible cure in ancient times, but today, they most definitely are not.

Like deadly nightshade, the more common black nightshade makes an excellent choice for cursing and tormenting the enemy, as its spirit, like its body, is possessed of both a poisonous and a tempting, alluring nature, drawing the enemy into its well-laid trap.

Burdock

(Arctium Lappa, Arctium Minus, Arctium Nemerosum,
and other related species)

Folk names: *Greater Burdock, Lesser Burdock, Fox's Clote, Thor's Mantle, Thorny Burr, Beggar's Buttons, Cockle Buttons, Love Leaves, Clot-Bur*
Regions: Common in most regions that experience freezing winters, though in differing varieties
Suggested Magical Uses: To "Catch" Offending Spirits or Persons; To Ward off Pests and Annoying Persons; To Strengthen or Break Bonds of Love or Friendship

The first word of the scientific name *arctium lappa* is derived from the Greek word for bear (*arktos*) and is said to denote the hairy, bristled appearance of the plant's burrs, which resemble smaller thistle heads. *Lappa* means "to seize," a quality for which the plant is quite famous, since the thistle heads have been tossed as a kind of game or amusing pastime to watch them stick and cling where they are thrown. This playful use of burdock was recorded even during the time of Shakespeare. Its common name today, *burdock*, is derived from the Latin *burra*, meaning a clump of wool, such as would be found clinging to its thistle heads in a field of sheep. The ancient Anglo-Saxon name for this plant, either *herrif* or *aireve*, most likely evolved from *hoeg* (a hedge) and *reafian* (to seize).

In the ancient world of Greece and Rome, the flowers of the burdock held the association of importunity, annoyance, and what we might today call "being clingy." Its Victorian associations, however, evolved to mean "touch me not" in the language of flowers. In some regions of the British Isles, there once existed various lore related to "catching" some small animal (often bats) by throwing the burrs at them and getting them to cling. Some older herbals indicate that the plant was at one time used in Albania as part of a ritual to exorcise evil spirits by smearing soggy bread, which had been soaked in wine, on the leaves of a burdock plant.

The folklore of this plant seems to revolve around two key properties: the chasing, clinging, or unrelenting pursuit, and the contrasting pattern of expulsion, deterrence, and defense. We can read the "push and pull" folkloric associations of this plant as an echo of its physical form, marked by both Venus and Mars, with its beautiful blooms and sharp barbs. It seems to lend itself readily to charms that have to do with bonds between friends or lovers—either to fortify them or to cast them asunder, in addition to dealing with pests and "catching" enemies that would prefer to hide or flee.

Buttercup

(Ranunculus Repens)

Folk names: *Crowfoot, King's Cup, Yellow Buttercup, Meadow Buttercup, Creeping Buttercup, Common Buttercup*
Regions: Common in most regions that experience freezing winters
Suggested Magical Uses: To Bring Prosperity; To Protect Against Theft; To Trick or Ensnare Others

Buttercup's scientific name, *ranunculus repens*, is derived from the Latin term for "little frog," most likely due to the plant's tendency to proliferate in moist areas where frogs are often numerous. The plant is recognizable for its bright yellow flowers in the spring, the petals of which have a distinctive gloss, causing them to shine in the sunlight. Despite the fact that buttercups are often associated with children's games, they are quite poisonous to both humans and animals, and ingesting them carries the risk of extreme gastrointestinal distress and possibly death.

In both the British Isles and North America, buttercup is most commonly associated with a children's game in which the shiny flower is held to one's chin. If the yellow of the flower reflects on the skin (which it often does when the sun is shining brightly), then it is said that one "likes butter." In Cornwall, buttercup was at one time rubbed on cow udders on May Day in order to ensure good milk production, and with the added purpose of deterring faeries from "stealing" the cow's milk. In older herbals, the plant is sometimes referred to as *king's cup* for its resemblance to the golden studs favored by royalty in previous eras. The old church's calendar of English flowers describes buttercup as "gilding" the land, emphasizing yet again its gold-like appearance.

While one does sometimes come across references to one particular tale involving buttercup, its origins are dubious, likely a work of children's fiction published as a "fairy story," a popular genre in the early 1900s. In the story, a miser who has hoarded much gold offends a group of faeries, who in turn transform all of his gold into buttercup flowers, distributing them across the land for all to enjoy. While amusing, this story is most likely fiction and not folklore.

Buttercup's relationship with the frog and with the dangers of poisoning clearly illustrate its saturnine properties, which lie in stark contrast to its quite solar appearance. This is one of many plants that contain a kind of riddle or paradox. The seemingly cheerful buttercup presents both reward and danger, capable of offering prosperity, but also concealing a hidden nature that is perhaps darker.

Catnip

(Nepeta Cataria)

Folk names: *Catnep, Catmint, Catrup, Cat's Wort, Cat's Delight, Cat's All-Heal*

Regions: Found often as an escaped garden plant self-propagating in regions that experience freezing winters

Suggested Magical Uses: To Bring Peace Where There Is Conflict (or vice versa); To Sharpen Perception; To Bring Intelligence and Mental Acuity; To Hide or Conceal One's Efforts

Just as the folklore of the lemon balm is thoroughly intertwined with the honeybee, so too is the folklore of catnip bound up in our feline companions. The fondness of cats for the crushed or bruised leaves of this plant has been documented for hundreds of years, distilled in a popular saying:

> "If you set it, the cats will get it;
> if you sow it, the cats won't know it."

Like many folk adages, there is a wisdom here, for a catnip plant that is grown from seed will not suffer the bruising and disturbance that is almost inevitable with transplanting, which releases the aroma that cats love so much, causing them to tear at and destroy the plant.

While most herbalists today would attest to catnip's mild anxiolytic and sedative properties, the old herbals note that it was once believed to have stimulating properties as well, and it was once enjoyed as an alternative to tea leaves imported from China. Folkard notes that catmint can cause those of calm, gentle dispositions to grow "quarrelsome" and fierce. As a mint, the plant does have a certain exhilarating aspect to its personality, but we must remember here that plant folklore and plant medicine, though sometimes overlapping, are distinct traditions, and the ferocity-inducing properties of catnip are most likely the result of folk knowledge of the plant's potencies from observing its relationship with felines. Although catnip is said to be disliked by rodents, there is perhaps a more obvious reason why rodents would not fare well living alongside a plant beloved by the local farm cat.

Both mercurial and venereal in its natures, catnip erupts in beautiful blooms favored by pollinators, and it releases an intoxicating scent that is at once clean, peppery, and sweet. Because of its close relationship with cats, the charmer would be wise to work with this plant spirit for its many cat-like characteristics, especially in workings of perception, intelligence, stealthiness, but also to quickly change the "mood" from peaceful to quarrelsome (or vice versa) in various persons or settings.

Chickweed

(Stellaria Media)

Folk names: *Starwort, Winterweed, Star Chickweed, Chickenwort, Chickenweed, Birdweed, Starweed*
Regions: Common in most regions that experience freezing winters
Suggested Magical Uses: To Fortify Familial or Group Bonds; To Bring Comfort and Soothe Suffering

Chickweed has long been associated with the spring and with renewal due to its uses as an early spring tonic for hundreds of years. Its folk names tend to echo three specific aspects of its nature: being associated with chickens and other birds, the night sky, and the cold months of the year.

That chickweed is generally known as a friendly, nourishing plant spirit should hardly come as a surprise. Chickens can be seen to forage for this herb at the first signs of spring, feasting on its crunchy, water-filled stalks and leaves in order to help their bodies recover from the long stint of winter, which usually provides little fresh vegetation. This plant's long association with chickens provides another key to its nature, for the common hen is a longstanding companion and ally to humans living in rural areas, offering eggs in exchange for protection and care. Most of us know the egg's associations with spring and with the vernal equinox, and as one of the first plants that stimulates the hen's system at winter's end, chickweed can be considered an ally in egg production.

Because chickweed plants tend to grow together in great, intertwined masses, it is sometimes associated with relationships and community. The fact that it is also beloved by hens, who live their entire lives surrounded by a tightly bonded flock, emphasizes, in my view, that the type of love embodied in this plant is more communal or familial than romantic. This is perhaps splitting hairs, though, since bonds of mutual care can express themselves in a variety of ways.

The older name for this herb, *starwort*, appears to be inspired by its pale flowers, which resemble small stars peeking out from the wet spring ground. Interestingly, the leaves are known to shift their posture by night, closing their leaves slightly around the tips of their stalks to protect new growth from frost, an adaptation well-suited to the cold environments in which it thrives. This may be the root of its occasional folk name *tongue grass*, though this name is also applied to other plants as well. This nocturnal movement and star-emblemed appearance suggest that this herb is possessed of a strong lunar nature, being an earthly reflection of the starry night sky that mirrors cycles of sleep. The juice-filled body of this herb has long been associated with comfort and soothing due to its myriad medicinal uses.

Chicory

(Cichorium Intybus)

Folk names: *Endive, Wild Endive, Cornflower, Blue Daisy, Blue Sailors, Blue Dandelion, Succory, Coffeeweed*
Regions: Common in most regions that experience freezing winters
Suggested Magical Uses: To Gain the Affection of Another; To Ensure Faithfulness and Fidelity; To Be Adored by Those in Power

Chicory, which is often referred to as *endive* or *succory* in older texts, is famous for its blue flowers, which open to the sun in the morning and close again at night. It has historically been eaten as a green, and the roots have been used as a kind of coffee. The vast majority of the chicory's lore, however, has to do with love and adoration.

Almost exactly like the plantain, there exists an old folktale in Germany and parts of the British Isles surrounding how the chicory was once a young woman who lost her lover and was doomed to live on as a chicory flower, waiting for his return beside the road. (Plantain and chicory are both common wayside plants, so this shared lore does make sense.) The seeds of the chicory were sold in previous ages by sorcerous folk as a love charm. In Rome, the chicory was uprooted carefully with a tool instead of the hand, so that one should not be exposed to its love-inducing properties accidentally. Carrying the root was said to ensure the faithfulness of one's lover.

The solar potencies of the chicory, though, are just as strong as its venereal ones, and it has been used since at least the times of Pliny the Elder to ensure the adoration of powerful persons, be they statesmen or colleagues. For this use, an oil of chicory was prepared, which would be applied to the skin before interacting with persons of authority.

Cinquefoil

(Potentilla Reptans, Potentilla Norvegica,
and related species)

Folk names: *Common Cinquefoil, Creeping Cinquefoil, Rough Cinquefoil, Norwegian Cinquefoil, Synkefoyle, Five-Leaf Grass, Five Fingers, Five-Finger Blossom, Sunkfield, Silverweed, Tormentil*
Regions: Common in most regions that experience freezing winters, usually in differing varieties
Suggested Magical Uses: To Achieve Mastery in One's Craft; To Rise to Stations of Power; To Bless with Health, Prosperity, and Love

The cinquefoil is actually a vast collection of related plants (all forms of potentilla), and the historically celebrated "five-leaf grass" is found in nearly every country that experiences cold in the winter. Its leaves grow in patterns of five, and its yellow flowers bear five large petals; this marking has given rise to all manner of associations with the five senses, the five fingers of the human hand, the five wounds of Christ, etc. In medieval times, it represented the mastery required by especially honored knights, and so it was used in heraldry as a symbol of high rank and honor. Its common name, *cinquefoil* (pronounced *sink-foil*), denotes *five leaves*.

It is interesting, then, that an herb so honored would be mentioned in old recipes for the much-fabled "witches' flying ointment" alongside baneful herbs like aconite. The five-leaf pattern may have contributed to the cinquefoil's association as a sorcerer's plant, as its form replicates the infamous Solomonic pentagram associated with the conjuration of spirits in the old grimoires. Although its occasional folk name *tormentil* may seem to imply baneful craft, this is a misunderstanding, as the *little torment* preserved in the name actually referred to the minor aches and pains for which cinquefoil was occasionally used in previous ages.

Sir Francis Bacon wrote that cinquefoil is much loved by frogs, a creature which, in addition to being an indicator of healthy soil and water, is also associated with sorcery and magic in general, being a sort of crosser of boundaries as it moves from water to land in its life cycle. The plant is also said to have been used in previous ages as a kind of love divination herb, much like the plantain or many other herbs used to predict the future spouse. Interestingly, it is mentioned in the grimoire *Le Petit Albert* as part of a prosperity charm to ensure a bounty of fish in one's net.

Much like Solomon's seal, we can view cinquefoil as a plant of *mastery*, bringing with it a variety of blessings of many different natures. This quality speaks to its jovial potencies. But from the form of its blooms, its association with healing, and its pentacle form, there is also a distinct impression of wholeness and the restoration of balance, from which I infer solar properties.

Clover

(Trifolium Repens, Trifolium Pratense, and related species)

Folk names: *Trefoil, Trifoil, Honeystalks, Purplewort, White Trefoil, Shamrock, Dutch Clover, Purple Clover, Sweet Clover, Heart Clover, Bee Bread*

Regions: Common in most regions that experience freezing winters, with other related "clover" species occurring nearly worldwide

Suggested Magical Uses: To Bring Dreams and Visions; To Perceive Spirits; To Bring Love; To Ensure Fidelity; To Protect Against Harmful Magics and Wicked Spirits; To Bring Luck and Good Fortune

The humble clover is most famous in two varieties: the red (which is actually a light purple) and the white. Both varieties are held to be in similar esteem since it is the leaf pattern and not the flower that concerns most of the folklore of the clover. The common name *trefoil* is derived from Latin, meaning "three leaves." The name *clover* comes from the Anglo-Saxon *cloefre*, meaning "club." The form of the three-leafed clover is actually the root of the clubs suit in the modern deck of playing cards, which is a note of interest to cartomancers, since this suit is often associated with treasures, possessions, and resources.

In the British Isles, the number of leaves on a particular stem of clover once determined its magical potency. The common three-leafed clover, which grows profusely in fields, holds prophetic powers, as it can be placed under one's pillow at night in order to dream of the future or placed in the shoe in order to protect oneself on a long journey. The triform clover is said to protect against baneful magics from witches and spirits. Its three leaves were said in ancient times to represent the earth, sea, and sky, while later, under Christianity, they came to represent the holy trinity.

Two-leafed clovers and four-leafed clovers are also said to possess unique magical properties, the two-leafed variety being used especially in love charms. A two-leafed clover placed under one's pillow was said to bring dreams of future love. Placed in the shoe of a lover, it was said to ensure fidelity. Even carrying the two-leafed clover was said to aid in finding true love.

The four-leafed clover, being a legendary magical charm known worldwide, is said to possess a variety of potencies, often to do with the fae. There is an old Cornish folktale of a maid who could not carry a large bucket of milk due to its weight, and so she placed clover upon her head in the hopes that the faeries would come to aid her, which they did. Their payment, though, was taken in the form of so many small sips of the milk that much of it was lost. The four-leafed clover is also said to grow where the fae have tread, preserving a portion of their magics, and enabling one to detect spirits otherwise imperceptible to the naked eye. The four-leafed clover is protective, guarding the possessor against curses and maleficia, and conferring excellent luck in all endeavors. It is sometimes said to be cruciform, resembling the holy cross, and thus conferring a more general blessing of success and favor in all matters.

It worth noting here that even the common three-leafed clover is possessed of strong magical potency. It is a favorite of rabbits, who will actively seek out fields of it in order to feast greedily on cool summer mornings. The hare, of course, is deeply connected with both the fae and with witches ourselves, as it was once believed that the spirit of the witch could travel forth at will in the form of a wild hare.

In Germany, there is said to be a wild "field spirit" that dwells in the clover which is called the *kleesau*, meaning the sow of the clover. That the sow is often connected with prosperity and good fortune can be no coincidence here. Clover is, practically speaking, an indicator of healthy soil composition and a source of sustenance for many forms of livestock, so its presence in agricultural communities is often a welcome one.

Generally speaking, the clover's heart shape and popularity with honeybees, which forage its blossoms all summer long, indicate a strong venereal nature, ossifying its relationship with matters of the heart and the general charming of others. Its three-leafed pattern, though, indicates a lunar nature as well, which relates to its role in dreams and visions. The fact that it is interpreted visually as a "club" echoes its martial properties, bringing protection and victory over challenges. Interestingly, the red variety of clover, among some Native American tribes, was once believed to grow where the blood of warriors had fallen, suggesting both a further connection with the potency of Mars and a connection with the realm of the dead. This, too, is no mere coincidence, since much of what is called the faery faith is actually a remembrance of a prehistoric cult of the dead.

Dandelion

(Taraxacum Officinale)

Folk names: *Piss-a-Bed, Wet-a-Bed, Lion's Tooth, Face Clock, Cankerwort, Blowball*
Regions: Common in most regions that experience freezing winters
Suggested Magical Uses: To Communicate with the Dead; To Bring Joy and Restore Mirth; To Divine Guidance; To Deter Enemies

Dandelion's folkloric associations are vast and quite old, and its myriad uses reveal this plant to possess a great many aspects, some of them seemingly paradoxical. Its properties tend to revolve, however, around a few central points: its associations with wish-making and divination, its surprising connection to both solar and saturnine powers, and its "toothed" properties as a protective plant.

The humorous names *piss-a-bed* and *wet-a-bed* are referenced in herbals as early as the 1600s, owing both to its diuretic properties and to the staining pigment in the bright, golden flowers. It is common even today for children to prank each other by rubbing the flower heads on one another's skin or clothing, resulting in a stain that doesn't really look much like urine, but makes them giggle nonetheless.

Vulgar names aside, dandelion's most commonly known use in folk magic stems from its round, tufted head of seeds that emerges after the flower has closed and matured. In folklore, the blowing of dandelion seeds (very much like the blowing of thistle seeds) is performed for a variety of purposes. When making a wish, the goal is to blow as many of the seeds as possible into the wind to encourage the desired outcome to take shape. In divination, the number of seeds left on the head after blowing is interpreted in a variety of ways: yes or no answers (many or few seeds remaining), the number of days until a specified event will occur, or the number of years left in one's life.

This last usage emphasizes an important aspect of dandelion's nature, being both a solar herb, possessed of the joyful and wholesome potencies of the Sun, and a saturnine one, associated with the chthonic realms and the spirits of the dead. While the dandelion's flowers mirror the form of the Sun, it grows a long and deep taproot, reaching into the dark earth below to a greater extend than other plants of its size. These roots twist and wind in a manner similar to mandrake. That this plant is an intermediary between realms is also signaled by its wind-blown seeds, which give away its mercurial and psychopompic qualities. Dandelion's personality is such an interesting contrast, being both joyful and macabre at the same time.

The very name *dandelion* is derived from the French *dent-de-lion*, referencing the tooth of a lion. This moniker is owed to the shape of its leaves, which are jagged in the manner of a cat's teeth.

Although its uses in contacting spirits, divining guidance, and wish-making are all well-known, this plant has a strong protective quality to it as well. We would do well not to mistake the dandelion's cheerful demeanor as being entirely passive (or toothless), as it is a magical plant with many uses, both gentle and fearsome.

Fleabane

(Erigeron Annuus, Erigeron Atticus,
and related species)

Folk names: *Common Fleabane, Daisy Fleabane, Job's Tears, Frostroot, Skervish, Robin's Plantain, St. Christopher's Herb*
Regions: Common in most regions that experience freezing winters
Suggested Magical Uses: To Repel Pests and Unwanted Persons; To Soothe Pain and Trauma; To Bring Serenity; To Fortify Boundaries; To Protect Against Danger

Fleabane refers not to a single plant, but to a great variety of members of the aster family, most recognizable for their small, tufted, sunflower-like blooms, with petals varying from white to lavender. This can be a difficult plant to identify since there are so many subspecies. One of the most common species in North America and the British Isles is erigeron annuus. While many common herbs in the United States actually originated in Europe, erigeron annuus has done the reverse, being a plant native to North America that has traveled and proliferated in the British Isles and elsewhere. Nonetheless, there exist many other native varieties of fleabane that are ubiquitous the world over.

In the medieval era, fleabane was frequently utilized as an insect repellant. The mild odor released when bruising the plant was believed to deter many insects, including fleas. The folk name *Job's tears* comes from an old bit of biblical lore; it is said that Job treated his sores and pustules during his period of torment using the flowers of the fleabane plant. In ancient Greece, it was said that the flowers of one variety of fleabane were used to prepare the beds of women participating in the Thesmophoria, a festival of Demeter and Persephone. The celebrants were considered "virgins," though the meaning in ancient Greece was quite different from the term's meaning today. Used in this sense, a *virgin* was simply a woman who did not desire a male partner. It is still believed in some parts of the British Isles and North America that placing fleabane around one's bed will deter fleas, though this is probably not the best modern solution to a flea infestation in one's home.

The flowers of erigerons clearly exhibit a solar nature, mirroring the shape and form of the Sun like other members of the aster family and communicating a joyful and wholesome personality. Solar potencies would certainly be at work in the old folktale of Job treating his wounds with the aid of this plant. Even so, since its most common historical use was as a pest deterrent, we cannot deny fleabane's martial properties, which may be useful to the modern practitioner dealing with any variety of "pests," in whatever form they may take. Fleabane's protective properties are distilled in its old folk name, *St. Christopher's Herb*, or sometimes simply *Christopher*, a saint believed to have carried a child across a dangerous river to safeguard his passage, only to find out later that the child was Christ himself.

Groundsel

(Senecio Vulgaris)

Folk names: *Old-Man-in-the-Spring, Ground Glutton, Sention, Simson, Grundy Swallow, Grundeswelge, Our Lady's Bed-Straw*

Regions: Common in most regions that experience freezing winters

Suggested Magical Uses: To Protect Against Curses; To Remove Unwanted Influences and Persons; To Mature and Age Gracefully

Groundsel was well-known only a few generations ago as a popular treat for caged birds, especially canaries and finches, who love eating it. It is, in fact, an ancient plant that has spread throughout the world wherever European grains were transported, likely due to its tufted, traveling seeds, which would have easily become mixed with seed and grain stores. It is somewhat similar in appearance to the sow thistle, but with daisy-shaped flowers like other members of the aster family. It is known to be toxic to both humans and livestock.

The common groundsel is sometimes called *old-man-in-the-spring* due to its white, tufted seed-heads, which become bald after a breeze blows away its "hair." In Scotland, it was also once called *grundy swallow*, which is itself derivative of *grundeswelge*, meaning *glutton of the ground*. This is likely due to its ability to rapidly proliferate, which has resulted in this plant being found nearly the world over. A jovial nature is certainly evident here, as with many other plants known for being fiercely prolific.

The plant also has a long history of use in folk magic. In Scotland, it was at one time considered a very effective highland charm against the evil eye and other curse-work of enemies and malefic witches. It was also used throughout the British Isles as a popular charm against fever, for which a sprig of it was worn against the bare skin. It is interestingly included among a few plants said to be a part of "Our Lady's Bed-Straw," the others being thyme and woodruff. These were said to be used to lay the bed for the newborn Christ-child. (We probably should not place a toxic plant in a child's bed, though.) The groundsel's martial, protective aspect is clear in these charms, and is echoed in its spear-shaped leaves.

While Pliny's ancient description of the plant includes a recommendation for use against toothache, we should take this passage as more folk-magical than medical. (And however we take it, we should never allow groundsel anywhere near our mouths, as it is actually considered poisonous.) He recommends severing a part of the root and transplanting it in the ground; if the new plant thrives, this supposedly indicates that all shall be well. This process is clearly a bit of sympathetic magic, for similar charms are known throughout the world, including the burying of onions that have been rubbed on wounds or warts in Appalachia, tree-boring in the Ozarks, and the driving of nails into trees and roots throughout the British Isles and parts of North America. Still, this association of "removal" is interesting here, as it echoes one of the defining features of this plant, which is its disappearing or "balding" seed head, a saturnine marking through and through. The seeds, of course, which travel on the wind, speak to mercurial properties lurking within.

Heather

(Calluna Vulgaris and related species)

Folk names: *Common Heather, Bog Heather, Blue Heather, Red Heather, Heath, Lyng, Ling, Scottish Heather*
Regions: Common in the British Isles and parts of North America, as well as other regions that experience freezing winters
Suggested Magical Uses: To Protect the Home; To Keep Secure One's Secrets and Treasures; To Make Contact with the Dead, Especially Ancestors; To Conquer Fear

Heather's associations with the pagan dead and the spirits of the otherworld are quite ancient. Though this plant is considered a cultural symbol of Scotland and Scottish heritage, it is also of great meaning and importance to Celtic cultures in general, as well as to Scandinavian cultures, where its reddish-purple flowers were said to represent the blood of fallen heathens or pagans. The very word *heather* shares the root of *heathen* and *heath*, this latter term indicating an ancient burial mound for the pagan dead. In Scotland and other Celtic countries, heather was said to grow on "faery hills," which is another way of referring to the same style of pagan burial mounds. Here, we must remember that the faery faith is, in many ways, a cult of the ancestral dead, and the faeries themselves are often the spirits of the pagan dead survived in a new and powerful form. Heather is also one of many plants noted to hide a "serpent stone" or a plant-veiled stone, which, if found, can be kept as a kind of talisman, according to Scottish lore.

One very famous folktale has to do with "heather ale," a brew said to be made with heather instead of hops by the ancient Picts. According to legend, a Viking king had slaughtered all but two Picts, a father and son, who were then brought before him and told that they must share the secret recipe for their delicious heather ale. To display his ferocity and instill obedience, the king killed the man's son outright, but this did not have the desired effect. The father remarked that his son was the only remaining Pict who would have been willing to share the secret recipe, and now that he was dead, the king would never possess it. In another version of this story, the father agrees to share the recipe if the king will grant his son a quick death, after which, he confesses that he knew his son would let the secret recipe slip if tortured, but with him dead, the secret was secure forever. In either version, one cannot help but admire the fearlessness of the Pictish father in this tale, who knows he is certain to face his death, but still takes pleasure in keeping the secret of his people from the enemy.

In Scotland, it was considered lucky to find the very rare white-flowered heather blooming in the highlands, and its flowers could be kept on the person as a kind of amulet. In Ireland, it was said that heather placed under a butter churn would prevent the butter being spoiled or stolen by the faeries. The ancient Irish king Conn-Ceud Chathach, or Conn of a Hundred Fights, was said to wear heather as a kind of badge.

Invariably, though, heather is widely known as a useful plant for making brooms, and it is still used for this purpose to this day. Stalks of heather are strong when dried, and this history of use resulted in heather being kept and hung in many homes, lending it an association of comfort, cleanliness, and security as well. That heather is also thoroughly associated with the ancient dead and their remembrance makes this a powerful plant for connecting to one's roots and drawing on the strength of those who have come before us.

Henbane

(Hyoscyamus Niger, Hyoscyamus Albus)

Folk names: *Black Henbane, White Henbane, Stinking Nightshade, Devil's Eye, Hogsbean, Cassilago, Cassilata, Hebenon, Henbells, Loaves of Bread, Insana*

Regions: Common throughout Europe and parts of North America

Suggested Magical Uses: To Curse the Enemy; To Torment with Nightmares; To Bring Madness; To Bring the Enemy's Efforts to Ruin; To Open Gates Between Worlds; To Receive Visions

Henbane comes in two varieties: the black and the white. Black henbane is the more common of the two, but both bear similar properties and lore. The plant grows long lines of flowers in a curved ladder form up its shoots, the blooms of which have an unpleasant odor, hence its occasional name *stinking nightshade*. All parts of the plant are considered lethally poisonous, with ingestion resulting in terrifying visions, coma, and death to humans and most animals. Its common name *henbane* comes from the observation of hens dying shortly after eating the plant's seeds.

In ancient times, the Greek spirits of the dead were said to be crowned with flowers of henbane in the underworld. The Romans considered henbane a plant of "ill omen," often found on tombs and old ruins. Interestingly, it is said that in Wales, the graves of old maids and old bachelors were sometimes overgrown with henbane. Like most nightshades, the henbane prefers recently disturbed soil, so in this case at least, its growth on graves is more likely to be a design in the plant's nature than a deliberate sowing of poisonous seeds by human hands as an insult to the dead. Henbane was also said to be worn by ancient Hebrew priests in their ceremonies, which is yet further evidence of its paradoxical nature.

In Germany, the henbane was said to bring sterility, rendering men impotent and women barren. Interestingly, it was also said to be used to bring rain. This ironic connection with both fertility and sterility reinforces henbane's witch-like nature, as witches were widely viewed as influencing crops, prosperity, and sexual reproduction, for good or ill. In Northern Italy, it was said that henbane juice, when sprinkled on a wild hare, would cause all other hares in the area to flee in terror. In Argentina, henbane was said to be used by witches to concoct a certain poison used to torment their victims with nightmares and horrific visions. *Le Petit Albert*, a folk-magical manual of the 1700s, lists henbane as an ingredient in a perfume of Saturn that is said to be appealing to certain spirits of the earth.

Almost invariably, though, henbane is preserved in folklore as the witches' herb par excellence, and its saturnine properties could not be clearer. It is included in the so-called "flying ointments" of early modern witch-lore, and it is named as a witch's poison in nearly all of the literature of this time. Despite its danger, its flowers and form are inarguably beautiful, and the veined petals of the black henbane speak to a certain loveliness even as they hint at the poison within. Its name *hogsbean* or *hogbean* comes from the once-popular belief that hogs adore the taste of it, but we should also note that the legendary witch-goddess Circe was said to transform offending men into hogs by her herbal arts. The symptoms of henbane poisoning are, after all, said to induce a kind of madness that turns men into animals. Perhaps something of the legendary Circe lingers here. Regardless, we should consider henbane a candidate for the most cruel of curses, but also for otherworldly journeying and the achievement of visions. This nightshade is a valuable spirit ally for witches, so long as we are careful not to harm ourselves in the process.

Honeysuckle

(Lonicera Periclymenum, Lonicera Xylosteum,
and related species)

Folk names: *Woodbine, Common Honeysuckle, European Honeysuckle, Fly Honeysuckle, Goat's Leaf*
Regions: Common throughout Europe and parts of North America, though local species may vary
Suggested Magical Uses: To Confer All Manner of Blessings; To Strengthen Bonds of Love; To Bring Peace, Comfort, and Serenity; To Ensnare Wicked Spirits and Spells of the Enemy

Honeysuckle, which is also called woodbine in the British Isles, has a long and complex history of magical use relating to benediction, healing, and love. In most cases, this lore revolves around its "embrace," echoing honeysuckle's tendency to grow in throngs, hugging trees or structures and releasing its intoxicatingly sweet scent in the surrounding area. Despite the famous pastime of children sucking the nectar from honeysuckle flowers, the berries of some varieties are mildly poisonous, causing gastrointestinal pain, vomiting, and possibly even more serious harm in some cases.

Some of the older herbals note a widespread charm to do with honeysuckle in previous ages in the British Isles, usually consisting of forming a circle of honeysuckle stalks and passing it over the patient from head to toe, after which the plant is burned. This is associated with the removal of various conditions. In Scotland, however, *girths* (or garlands) of the plant were said to be used by witches to confer blessings by passing the patient through it nine times while certain charms were spoken. The fact that so many spoken "counting charms" survive in Scottish folk-magical practice (some examples of which can be found in the *Carmina Gadelica*) is no coincidence, but evidence that this form of craft was most likely quite widespread in previous ages.

In French tradition, the honeysuckle is associated with deep, devoted love and fidelity, and at one time it was commonly presented as a token of such affection to one's sweetheart. Interestingly, it was also commonly planted in French cemeteries, presumably to surround the tombs of the dead with this symbol of affection and to fill the resting place of loved ones with the honeysuckle's miasma of sweetness. While the superstitions surrounding plants near graves often have dark connotations in British and American folklore, this relic of French lore seems to bear more tenderness, relying on this benevolent plant spirit to encircle the beloved dead.

In Germany, the honeysuckle or woodbine is sometimes given the name *albranke*, meaning "witch's snare." (A snare, of course, is a trap set by hunters that is usually circular in form, resembling a girth or wreath.) One Italian variety of honeysuckle, named *caprifoleum*, is actually named for its association with goats, for it was once said that the plant could be found in high places that only goats could reach, hence the popular name "goat's leaf." In both of these cases, we see the tempting and alluring properties of honeysuckle emphasized, the scent of which charms both beasts and the spirits of malefic witches with its sweetness.

The distinct fragrance of its flowers clearly signals the influence of Venus in this plant, but in its rapid proliferation and great throngs of growth, I also read a certain jovial potency, which would make sense, considering its associations with good fortune, blessings, and health. In the charmer's arts, honeysuckle is an excellent choice for any of these arts, as well as for workings that require a kind of bait designed to mesmerize and draw in unwanted influences so that they may be trapped and expelled.

Lemon Balm

(Melissa Officinalis)

Folk names: Balm, Honey balm, Honey blossom, Sweet balm, Bee balm, Common balm, Melissa balm, Melissa
Regions: Southern Europe, originally, though now naturalized throughout much of the world as an escaped garden plant
Suggested Magical Uses: To Persuade Others to Follow Your Leadership; To Sweeten Dispositions; To Charm Animals

Most of our lore concerning lemon balm comes to us from classical times, hearkening back to its close relationship with the honeybee, which has long been considered a sacred creature. Belonging to the mint family, the plant emits a pleasant, lemony odor when bruised and is well-known for its delicate flavor in tea. Its flowers are beloved by bees. If hearty enough, the roots will become perennial, though the plant will wither away each year. Melissa generally grows up to two feet high, bearing white or cream-colored flowers at the base of its stems.

The very name *Melissa* appears in ancient mythology as the name of a nymph who first discovered and taught human beings how to procure and use honey. Curiously, the name *Melissa* also appears to be the name given to ancient priestesses of Demeter and Persephone. Some writers have suggested that the name *Melissa* is related to the title *Melittodes*, an old epithet used for both goddesses, through the root word *meli*, or honey, so named for the songs sung by the ancient priestesses. This is also quite plainly related to the Latin root of our modern word *melody*.

It has been said that the plant, when placed in an empty hive, will draw a new colony of bees to take up residence. On a related note, there exists an old superstition that one can lead cattle wherever one wishes when carrying lemon balm. It is no coincidence, then, that in the old legends, the Athenians journeyed to found their first colony in Ionia by following a procession of honeybees, these very creatures being a form chosen by the muses themselves.

The honeybee is, of course, a well-known pollinator, ensuring the survival of so many plants and trees. It also provides honey, which not only nourishes, but heals. Its sweetness is distinct and quickening. All of these qualities are reflected in this herb, which has since antiquity been associated with healing, comfort, joy, music, the charming of beasts, and the sweetening of dispositions.

Lemon balm's magical signatures are complex. Its sweet scent clearly aligns it with Venus, though its pale blossoms and sleep-inducing qualities also suggest a lunar nature. The venereal aspect of this herb is reflected in its folklore and superstitions, in which it is suggested that bees and other creatures may be lulled into submission through its use. Culpeper describes its healing properties as belonging to Jupiter, saying that the plant "strengthens nature much in all its actions." We should also consider, though, the important role of the female spirits associated with this plant, as well as its connection to the honeybee colony, which is a matriarchal society of sisters who tend to their queen.

Mallow

(Malva Sylvestris and related species)

Folk names: *Common Mallow, High Mallow, Tall Mallow, Cheese Flower, Cheeses, Blue Mallow, and others*
Regions: Common in most regions that experience freezing winters, as well as in some tropical regions
Suggested Magical Uses: To Fortify and Strengthen; To Protect Against All Harm; To Bring Aid in Time of Need

While the "high mallow" or *malva sylvestris* is more limited to regions with freezing winters, some form of mallow is present in nearly any part of the world, this being an ancient plant with a long history of use. Certain historical species were considered edible and nourishing, and the mallow is noted to have been eaten in Ancient Egypt, Syria, and Rome. In the British Isles, the mallow's fruit was sometimes referred to as "cheeses" by children, who noted its cheese wheel-like shape.

The fact that the fiber of the mallow plant can be made into fabric, coupled with its umbrella-like leaves, perhaps suggest an important part of its nature: protection from harm. Mallow was believed in ancient times to guard against diseases, but also against curse work. In German folk magic, an ointment made from mallow was once said to protect against all manner of danger. In old May Day celebrations, mallow flowers were once used to decorate doorways, a use shared by other plants with warding or protective potencies. Interestingly, mallow is said to have been used in the funerary customs of ancient Greece and planted on graves, perhaps with the magical aim of nourishing or protecting loved ones after death.

Some types of mallow flowers have been known to close at night, and the plant is often associated with solar properties for this reason, but its nourishing and gentle qualities also reveal strong venereal tendencies. Because the mallow plant yields a thick, viscous liquid in medicinal preparations, its history of use has established the plant's associations with soothing and gentle aid.

Mint

(Mentha Aversis, Mentha Spicata,
and related species)

Folk names: *Wild Mint, Corn Mint, Field Mint, Spearmint, Common Mint,* and others, depending on species
Regions: Common in its wild form in most regions, especially in creeks or very wet soil
Suggested Magical Uses: To Clear Away That Which Is Foul; To Comfort the Grieving Heart; To Lift Up the Downtrodden; To Cause or Ease Jealousy

Wild mint and spearmint, despite being distinct species, share quite similar qualities, both being favored for their "clean" scent when bruised and both having an extensive history of use in cuisine and fragrances. Older herbals note that the odor of mint stimulates the mind, but can be disastrous when applied to open wounds. (This is due to the oils of the mint plant, which can be very irritating to sensitive areas or even those with sensitive skin in general).

The lore of the ever-popular mint is, in fact, very ancient and tied to the underworld. It was once said that the mint was a nymph named Minthe, a minor goddess who resided in the realm of the dead. She was the daughter of a river god, and she was, for a time, the concubine of Hades himself, a tryst for which she was punished (either by a jealous Persephone or an enraged Demeter, depending on the tale) by being transformed into the plant we know as mint. Some renditions of this myth note that Hades boasted how Minthe was more beautiful than any goddess, a clear insult to Persephone as the goddess of both the dead and the flowers of spring. In some versions, Demeter is said to "trample" the nymph Minthe, which is interesting, since it is the bruised plant that releases the strong fragrance we associate with mint.

Elements of this tale relate to the plant's ancient history of use as a funerary aromatic, hiding the scent of corpses, as well as its use in entheogenic drinks associated with the ancient religious cults of Persephone and Demeter. For anyone who has ever come across a patch of wild mint growing in a shady creek, one cannot help but be enchanted by the mythic portrayal of Minthe as the daughter of a river god dwelling in the darkness of the underworld, for this is exactly the nature of at least one aspect of this spirit in its wild form, drenched in cool water and soft shadow.

We can easily discern the mercurial aspect of this plant from its energizing scent, which is bright and quickening, being used for oral hygiene even in ancient times. It is also somewhat venereal, depending on the species, which can sometimes have attractive flowers and a somewhat sweet fragrance. Due to its ancient lore, though, we cannot deny its saturnine properties and its relationship with the dead and the realm of the dead. Its uses in magical practice may include clearing away that which is foul, comforting the grief-stricken, uplifting the downtrodden (i.e., those who have been "trampled), or even causing or releasing jealousy.

Mugwort

(Artemisia Vulgaris)

Folk names: *Felon's Herb, St. John's Plant, Muggons, Old Uncle Henry, Cronewort, Sailor's Tobacco*

Regions: Common in most regions that experience freezing winters

Suggested Magical Uses: To Incite Visions or Dreams; To Achieve Spirit Flight or Journeying; To Protect Against Harm; To Protect Against Weariness

Mugwort has a very long history of use dating back to prehistoric times. Its name has been suggested to be derived from "mug," referring to its use as a flavoring in beer before the use of hops. Alternately, some sources suggest the root of its name comes from *moughte*, referring to a moth or maggot. This could also be true, since mugwort was used in ancient times to deter insects. Mugwort, like wormwood, contains the chemical thujone, and it shares some properties with old-style absinthe. Because of this, internal use may be harmful for some individuals. Mugwort's strong association with women's medicine, preserved in its old folk name of "cronewort," has to do with its reported ability to stimulate menstruation when taken internally.

The herb's folk name, "St. John's Plant," carries an interesting bit of history, as mugwort was strongly associated with St. John in medieval times, and it was commonly believed that John the Baptist wore a girdle of mugwort during his wandering through the wilderness. This gave way to much folk-magical use involving protection from any number of dangers, both physical and spiritual. This protective aspect of mugwort is echoed in its spear-shaped leaves (suggestive of its martial nature), which are green on one side and a shimmering silver on the other. This sheen is due to many very small hairs on the underside of the leaves. Nor can we ignore the saturnine properties of this plant, for when a large throng of mugwort is left to grow as it will, it forms a dense, thick, entangled system of roots that can be very difficult to remove.

The association with John the Baptist may also be the root of the herb's frequent association with journeys and travel. In the time of Rome, Pliny wrote of mugwort's ability to protect against weariness when travelling, and in the 1600s, Coles wrote that a leaf of mugwort, when placed in the shoe, would allow a man to journey forty miles before noon and not be weary.

In modern magical usage, though, mugwort is most commonly associated with increasing one's ability to receive dreams and visions, including loosening the spirit that one might more easily achieve spirit flight or experience otherworldly journeying. This is due partly to the herb's use in beer and its properties similar to wormwood (though its inebriating effects are extremely mild, in my own experience), but also due to its association with lunar currents (note the name *artemisia*). But even among other transvective herbs, mugwort is unique for its simultaneous ability to protect the practitioner during spiritual travel, a potency for which it is much adored by witches and pagans today.

Mullein

(Verbascum Thapsus and related species)

Folk names: *Common Mullein, Great Mullein, Greater Mullein, Hag-Taper, Hag's Taper, Candlewick, Torch Plant, Flannel Plant, Our Lady's Flannel, Jupiter's Staff, Jacob's Staff, Aaron's Rod, Light of the Lord*

Regions: Common in North America, Southern England, and most regions that experience freezing winters

Suggested Magical Uses: To Reveal Hidden Things; To Bring Great Blessings; To Illuminate Darkness; To Resist Compelling Charms

Mullein is most well-known for its long stalk, which bears its prolific seed-heads. It is an extremely prolific plant, having spread nearly the world over, though it occurs in many different varieties depending on the region. Its many names relating to fire and light (*candlewick, light of our lord, torch plant, hag's taper,* etc.) have been interpreted to signify many things, but universally, it has been observed that the long stalks of the mullein make for excellent kindling.

In the British Isles, the plant was once called hag's taper due to the belief that witches and warlocks used the stalks of the plant as candles in magical rites. Interestingly, the ancient Romans once called the plant *candelaria*, and it was used as a torch during funerary rites by dipping its long stalk in animal fat. It later bore the name *light of our lord* in Italy, preserving its history of use in a new moniker. If one wishes to experiment with luminary rites using the mullein plant, I recommend the use of a mullein-infused oil to dress a taper, since lighting large stalks of dried herb can produce a very unpredictable flame.

In most European cultures, mullein holds the association of warding, and is known to keep wicked spirits and magical practitioners at bay. Some old herbals note the historic use of mullein candles in old churches at times when wax candles were scarce. This has probably given rise to its many biblically-themed names, including *our lady's flannel, Jacob's staff,* and *Aaron's rod.* The protective powers of the mullein plant are also quite ancient in origin, for the plant is often interpreted as the one used by Ulysses in order to overcome the witchcraft of Circe.

The light-bearing qualities of this plant are a clear signifier of its solar nature, but its tall and towering appearance in the field, coupled with its prolific seed-heads, also speaks to a jovial potency that lies within, making mullein an excellent candidate for workings of benediction, illumination, and the hallowing of spaces and persons. Its occasional associations with the dead and with dark magics can be read here in a sanctifying capacity since mullein's nature seems to bless and shed light on various forms of unwanted darkness.

Plantain

(Plantago Major, Plantago Lanceolata,
and related species)

Folk names: *Common Plantain, Broad-leafed Plantain, Ribleaf Plantain, Waybread, Waybroad, Cuckoo's Bread, Ripple Grass, Snakeweed, Englishman's Foot, White Man's Footprint, Kemps, and others, depending on species*

Regions: Common in most areas that experience freezing winters

Suggested Magical Uses: To Bring Strength and Endurance; To Repel Wicked Spirits and Malefic Magics; To Heal Pain and Trauma; To Divine the Future

There are few herbs both as celebrated and as common as the plantain, this plant being distributed throughout most parts of the world. Plantain is well-known for its ability to tolerate rocky and compacted soils, growing even amidst gravel or cracks in stone and cement. It is so hardy that it even survives trampling, a quality for which it has been famous since ancient times. It is often found roadside, where it thrives in conditions that other plants cannot withstand.

Plantain is mentioned in the 10th century *Lacnunga*, a book of Anglo-Saxon charms, as being potent against "poison" and "the flying poison," which is to say, bodily harm and spiritual harm caused by malefic witchcraft. (The language of the *Lacnunga* has been translated, alternatively, to mean "flying *venom*," denoting spiritual harm accomplished via the arts of ekstasis and transvection, the transvective sorcerer long being associated with serpents.) The association of plantain with the strength of a warrior extends, in Scotland and elsewhere, to its use in children's games, mimicking soldiers at war by slapping the long heads of plantain stems against one another to see which "head" comes off first. The ribwort plantain is also referred to as *kemps*, a term with Anglo-Saxon roots referring to a soldier. Plantain's fortifying potency was, like many healing herbs, interpreted through both the lenses of bodily wellness and spiritual wellness. Plantain's history of use reveals its potency as a healing aid, being applied in the past (and even today) to bruises and insect bites to speed healing.

Its names *waybread* and *waybroad* are derived from its tendency to grow along waysides (roadsides). This relates to an old bit of folklore found in Germany and some parts of the British Isles that the plantain was once a human maiden who waited so long beside the road for her lover to return, that she became a plant. (This tale is echoed in the lore of the chicory plant, as they both frequently grow along roadsides.) Once every seven years, she is said to take the form of a cuckoo, singing out in her loneliness. This relates well to the plantain's use in love charms, for in England, it was once believed that there was a hidden stone beneath the plantain that could be placed under a young woman's pillow that she might dream of her future husband. As with other magics used by young women to divine a spouse, we should not take this charm lightly, for a young woman's choice of husband in previous ages was a dire decision that would shape not only her love life, but her lifestyle, her political affiliations, her prosperity, her personal freedoms (or lack thereof), and her treatment in the community. We should read the divination of one's husband as the divination of all of these things, for a woman's choice of spouse in previous ages was tied to survival in many ways.

The common plantain's lengthy seed-stalk, which helps it proliferate so abundantly, reveals some of its jovial properties, while its milky sap speaks to lunar currents at work beneath the surface. As with many plants, its planetary potencies are quite mixed, for we could easily read its ability to grow in relatively dry, hot soil as expressing a solar nature as well. Plantain can be read as a well-rounded spirit ally, often one of the first plants charmers encounter when learning their local flora, and an eager helper along the path.

Prickly Lettuce

(Lactuca Serriola)

Folk names: *Wild Lettuce; Compass Plant; Scarole; Wild Opium*
Regions: Common in most areas that experience freezing winters
Suggested Magical Uses: To Sustain or Ruin Love; To Overcome Infatuation; To Release Grief; To Achieve Visions or Dreams of the Otherworld; To Contact the Dead

Prickly lettuce has a complex history of both use and lore, being adored during certain ages and reviled during others. Invariably, it is associated with matters of love and desire, but it is also often associated with stilling and arresting processes, bringing rest and repose or death and infertility. The plant seems, too, to have a strong connection to cyclical processes; its folk name *compass plant* comes from the tendency of its uppermost leaves to shift their posture to face the sun.

In classical times, the prickly lettuce, as well as other, related species of wild lettuce, was used frequently for its mild sedative and analgesic properties, which were said to be somewhat euphoric. The latex sap that exudes from the plant somewhat resembles the latex of the poppy, hence its occasional name *wild opium*. Apuleius wrote that the eagle, when he wished to fly high and see far, would pluck the wild lettuce from the ground, and in ancient Greece, the prickly lettuce was both an offering to the dead and a food served at funerary gatherings.

Most famously, though, there is the ancient tale of Aphrodite, goddess of love, and her mortal lover, Adonis, which is thoroughly connected with the wild lettuce. Adonis was said to be the most beautiful man in the world, and when the goddess of love sought to hide him in a bed of wild lettuce, a boar came to eat of it and killed him, and he died in her arms shortly after. He is afterwards, in various myths, raised to immortality. This sacrificial god myth bore an ancient cult, and it is widely believed today to be descended from the ancient cults of Inanna or Ishtar and her lover Dumuzid. Some folklorists have noted the likeness of sacrificial gods, who die and rise again, to the cycles of vegetation. In the case of Adonis and the wild lettuce, this can be no coincidence.

In medieval England, it was said that an evil spirit dwelled within patches of wild lettuce, and great care must be taken not to disturb it and incur its wrath. The prickly lettuce was associated with sterility in men and barrenness in women, in some ways echoing the ancient tale of doomed love between the goddess and her chosen consort.

Ragwort

(Jacobaea Vulgaris, Packera Anonyma,
and other species)

Folk names: *Fairy's Horse, Common Ragwort, Tansy Ragwort, Stinking Willie, Stinking Nanny, St. James Wort, Staggerwort, Cankerwort, Small's Ragwort, Appalachian Ragwort*

Regions: Common in most areas that experience freezing winters, though varieties may differ by region

Suggested Magical Uses: To Begin Journeys; To Connect with the Spirits of the Fae and the Dead; To "Send" Various Things on Their Way; To Cause Nightmares

Ragwort's association with faeries, witches, and the nocturnal flights of otherworldly beings is distilled in the old Scottish quote, "as rank a witch as ever rode ragwort." The stalks of most varieties of ragwort grow quite tall, topped with golden, daisy-like flowers that signal its place in the aster family. Though it was prescribed as a remedy for both livestock and humans in previous ages, it is now known to be poisonous to both.

In Scotland, Ireland, and Cornwall, the plant is known as *fairies' horse* or *fairy's horse*, and folklore abounds regarding the nocturnal flight of faeries and witches upon the stems of flowering ragwort. In Ireland, ragwort was said to be beloved by leprechauns, and it was believed that this particular variety of faery would hide a treasure under a ragwort plant. (This is one of many hints at the plant-veiled stone as a folk-magical talisman.) We should always remember, though, when speaking of the Good People, that they are in many ways the ancestral spirits of the dead in Celtic cultures, and so the "treasure" of the leprechaun is, in a less literal sense, not one to be uncovered, but one related to the chthonic realms of the dead, signifying once again the ragwort's properties as a liminal or boundary-crossing plant.

The name *St. James wort* is usually said to be applied to this plant due to the role of St. James as the patron saint of horses. Ragwort was prescribed frequently in older herbals for horses and other livestock, particularly for diseases that affected their walking (hence the name *staggerwort*). It was quite a long time before ragwort was discovered to be poisonous to livestock and to humans, this being largely due to the slow, cumulative nature of the poisoning, which would build in the body over a period of time and present symptoms slowly rather than all at once after ingestion.

Ragwort is obviously most useful to the charmer as a transvective plant or magical vehicle, capable of bringing the practitioner between worlds as a kind of otherworldly steed or, in effect, "carrying" things or persons on various journeys. Its poisonous nature and associations with the fae cannot be ignored, though, as these both speak to saturnine potencies that can be quite dark in nature, even bordering on malevolent, a hidden aspect that stands in stark contrast to the ragwort's sunny flowers. We should remember that the folkloric "witch's ride" is sometimes itself associated with baneful craft, as in the "hag-riding" of Appalachian lore, in which the victim's spirit is transformed into a horse and used for a steed, often remembered later as "nightmares." The journey offered by the spirit of the ragwort it likely useful for some and disastrous for others, depending on our relationship with the spirits after whom the "fairy horse" is named.

Shepherd's Purse

(Capsella Brusa-Pastoris)

Folk names: *Shepherd's Bag, Lady's Purse, Pickpocket, Pickpurse, St. James' Wort, Poor Man's Parmacetty, Toywort, Caseweed, Mother's Heart, Pepper Plant, Witch's Pouch, Poor Man's Pepper*
Regions: Common in most regions that experience freezing winters
Suggested Magical Uses: To Bring Prosperity; To Steal the Good Fortune of Another; To End Relationships; To Cause Heartbreak

Shepherd's purse is most well-known for its seed pouch, which resembles a tiny, triangular purse or coin bag. This has given rise to many of its folk names, including *pickpurse, pickpocket,* and *witch's pouch*. In the British Isles and parts of North America, it is said that these names relate to the plant's proliferation as a nuisance on farms, stealing the "goodness" of the land, but I find it more likely that it relates to the form of the seed pod itself. The seeds have been reported to taste somewhat like black pepper. These folkloric associations make the herb an excellent choice for matters of prosperity as well as the "theft" of another party's good fortune. The plant's very fine and particulate anatomy, which appears to shiver in the breeze, reveals its mercurial potencies.

The name *mother's heart* is interesting here, and it relates to a children's game in the British Isles of attempting to pinch the heart-shaped seed pouch without breaking it, which is quite difficult. At the moment of failure, it is pronounced that one has "broke your mother's heart." Because the form of the pouch so resembles the symbol of the heart, shepherd's purse can be said to have a venereal nature as well, and the plant is well-suited to workings of heartbreak and the "severing" of bonds.

Solomon's Seal

(Polygonatum Biflorum, Polygonatum Multiflorum,
and related species)

Folk names: *Lady's Seal, Seal-Wort, Seal-Root, White Root, Jacob's Ladder, Ladder-to-Heaven, Mary's Seal, Drop-Berry, David's Harp*

Regions: Common in North America and often found as a garden escapee in the British Isles

Suggested Magical Uses: To "Seal Together" People or Things; To Bring Divine Protection; To Open Gates Between Worlds; To Achieve Magical Mastery; To Receive Visions of the Otherworld

Though Solomon's seal somewhat resembles the lethally poisonous lily of the valley, the plant has a long history of use in the herbal healing arts. It is usually noted to be poisonous at least in part, the toxins being most concentrated in the berries. Despite this, Solomon's seal is recommended in old herbals for treating a great variety of ailments, including broken bones and open wounds. It was, in previous ages, said to "seal" wounds and broken bones back together. While better medical approaches exist today, the magical meaning of this interpretation has woven itself deeply into the lore of this plant. Its rhizome form, which resembles many appendages held together by a series of joints (hence the name *polygonatum* or "many knees"), echoes this property of bringing disparate elements into unity.

There is some debate as to the origins of its popular name, but most experts believe it is called Solomon's seal after the six-pointed star shape revealed when cutting its root, this symbol being associated with the magical arts of the legendary sorcerer Solomon, who was said to possess the secret knowledge of all herbs and plants. For the charmer, this form is no mere accident of nature, but a symbol of the plant's fitness for magical work ingrained in its very shape. The root of the plant, which is like a hand stretched into the otherworld, bears the star familiar to many varieties of cunning craft and other folk-magical traditions, being a symbol of protection, transcendence, and magical mastery.

The above-ground form of this plant is surrounded by its own lore as well. The biflorum variety, which develops small flowers lined up in a kind of arched ladder, has given way to the names *Jacob's ladder* and *ladder-to-heaven*. Some species also grow into a form resembling medieval illustrations of the biblical poet David sitting at his harp, which has given way to the name *David's harp*. Even outside of conventional Christianity, we can read these attributes as signaling the plant's ability to conduct and transmit potent spiritual energy from the otherworld.

Its drop-shaped flowers clearly indicate a lunar nature at work in this plant, which makes good sense. Both the "ladder to heaven" and the "harp of David" are emblematic of visionary, transportive experiences that fit well under the domain of the Moon. Its somewhat poisonous nature, however, gives away its saturnine properties, even if its history of use in healing speaks to a certain solar potency. This is a complex plant that should be approached with care, but considered as a candidate for protective charms, the opening of gates, and the "sealing together" of various things.

Sow Thistle

(Sonchus Oleraceus and related species)

Folk names: *Sowthistle, Hare's Colwort, Hare's Thistle, Hare's Palace, Hare's Lettuce, Milky Tassel, Smooth Thistle, Soft Thistle*

Regions: Common in most areas that experience freezing winters

Suggested Magical Uses: To Strengthen One Against Adversity; To Divine Guidance; To Protect from Harm; To Bring Prosperity

While sow thistle can be said to share many properties with other forms of thistle that have likewise proliferated the world over, it is distinct in its associations with nourishment, fortification, good fortune, and prosperity. The flowers of the sow thistle appear quite similar to dandelion flowers, and like dandelion (and like most other thistles), these flowers erupt into tufted seed-heads that distribute the next generation of plants on the breeze. The prickly leaves of the sow thistle are softer than other thistle plants, being much easier to approach and handle.

The name *sow thistle* comes from pigs being observed to eat greedily of this plant when it is available. The names *hare's thistle* and *hare's palace* denote the love that hares also have for this plant, one of its favorite sources of nourishment observed in previous ages.

The 1500s text *Grete Herball* describes how the sow-thistle is sometimes referred to as *hare's palace*, owing to the fact that a hare taking shelter beneath it is under the thistle's protection.

From Italy, there comes a great deal of lore attached to the sow thistle. It was once used to decorate mangers for Christmas. Even more interestingly, it is preserved in the exclamation "Open, sow thistle," which appears folklorically as a phrase similar in manner to "Open, sesame." It was once said that the sow thistle holds the power to reveal hidden treasures.

The aspect of sow thistle related to prosperity has perhaps a darker side, but this should not surprise us, for the power to locate hidden treasures is often, at least partially, connected with the beings of the otherworld and the spirits of the dead. According to Pliny, it was Hecate, goddess of witchcraft, the dead, and the wilderness, who offered King Theseus a dish of sow thistle to strengthen him before his battle with the Marathonian Bull. Some sources note that this may be a confusion of the name Hecate for *Hecale*, but this point is perhaps moot, since Theseus is by any measure a hero-god operating under the favor of Hecate, who supplies him with other aid when he famously faces the minotaur.

In Russia, the sow thistle is said to belong to the Devil, a dark bit of lore that is sometimes seen with other types of thistle as well. Like other forms of thistle, the sow thistle is said to belong to the group of plants known as "flower clocks." Its tufted seeds are blown on the wind—much like the dandelion or scotch thistle—so that the remaining number of seeds may be counted to divine the days or hours until a certain event occurs.

For the charmer, this gentler form of thistle has a more strengthening and fortifying quality, a solar nature echoed in the form of its flowers. Its windborne seeds of course denote mercurial qualities. Its associations with hares, sows, Hecate, and the otherworld also denote some saturnine and lunar connections as well.

Star of Bethlehem

(Ornithogalum Umbellatum and related species)

Folk names: *Garden Star-of-Bethlehem, Star-o-Bethel, Nap-at-Noon, Eleven-o'clock-Lady, Grass Lily, Sleepy Dick, Summer Snowflake, Dove's Dung, Bath Asparagus, Star of Hungary*
Regions: Common in most regions that experience freezing winters
Suggested Magical Uses: To Bring a Restorative Peace; To Give Hope; To Fortify Oneself or Others When Facing Long Struggles

Star of Bethlehem blooms in late spring to early summer. Its pale white flowers resemble a six-pointed star, and when the plant flowers in great droves, as it tends to do in the spring, its carpet bed of white blossoms is truly magical to behold. Magically, we can approach this plant as a bearer of hope for good things to come, an ally in times of duress, and a bringer of restorative peace in the midst of chaos, but despite its benevolent properties, it is considered poisonous today and should be approached with caution.

The name *star of Bethlehem* is a very obvious reference to the star signaling the birth of Christ in Christian tradition, but we can read the star of Bethlehem as offering hope for the future in more general terms, this being a flower of spring that signals the coming arrival of summer's warmth. Dierbach's *Flora Mythologica* notes that the flower held the symbolism of purity in classical times. One popular folktale recounts how, at Christ's birth, the star of

Bethlehem fell to earth, shattering into many pieces, which rose up as the pale flowers we recognize today.

Because the flowers of the star of Bethlehem do not open until late morning (often said to be precisely 11 o'clock), the plant is sometimes called *sleepy dick, nap-at-noon,* or *eleven-o'clock-lady.* The nature of its flowers seems to remind us not to exert ourselves unnecessarily and to allow ourselves to be rested and restored for important work that may be yet to come.

The history behind its name *dove's dung* is very interesting, for the star of Bethlehem is said to be the food source mentioned by this name in the Old Testament as a crop eaten during famine times. Due to the dove's ancient association with holiness and the fact that their waste falls to earth, we see here echoes of the folktale of the star falling to earth in a more biological way. Despite the fact that older herbals frequently mention the edibility of this plant, most varieties of star-of-Bethlehem found today are actually quite poisonous, causing gastrointestinal distress and even skin irritation. It is sad to consider, but also quite possible that many plants that were edible or medicinal in ancient times have now become toxic due to environmental destruction. One wonders whether the "purity" of the star of Bethlehem has changed somehow in response to human actions.

Despite its toxicity, I find this ancient, legendary plant to be an amiable plant spirit, mingling solar and lunar potencies in its makeup, balancing currents of restoration and fortification with currents of dreaminess, wish-making, and hopes for the future.

Teasel

(Dipsacus Fullonum, Dipsacus Sylvestris,
and related species)

Folk names: *Teazle, Tezil, Common Teasel, Fuller's Teasel, Fuller's Thistle, Wild Teasel, Venus Basin, Card Thistle, Barber's Brush, Church Broom, Brushes and Combs*

Regions: Common in most regions that experience freezing winters

Suggested Magical Uses: To Soften Unyielding Dispositions; To Beguile and Charm Others; To Lay a Lingering, Though Milder Curse

The name *teasel* comes from the Anglo-Saxon *taesan*, meaning to tease cloth in order to raise its nap. This historic use was very widespread, even up to only one hundred years ago. The dried thistle-like burr heads were used against the weave of fabrics in order to cause their fibers to soften and loosen slightly on the surface of the cloth, resulting in a softer, thicker fabric. A *fuller* was, likewise, a professional who worked with cloth. The name *church broom* may suggest that the barbed head was, in previous ages, useful for cleaning dust and gathered debris.

The name *Venus basin* is interesting and relates to an old bit of folklore surrounding the plant's physiology. The base of the teasel's leaves, which wrap closely around the stem, form little cups or basins that often fill with water after a rain. This water was once said in many parts of the British Isles to be beautifying to the face. In Ireland, it was said to be water belonging to the faeries. Teasels have been observed to collect nutrients from dead insects drowned in these "Venus basins," and so it is sometimes considered a "proto-carnivorous" plant. Teasel's venereal nature is clear in this capacity, but I suspect that its potency in this aspect of Venus is more favorable for works of deception and manipulation than actual love.

In the old *English Dictionary of Flowers*, teasel is given the sentimental association of misanthropy. This echoes its occasional association as a nuisance plant, for the barbs cling to clothing when walking by, and its prickles are quite sharp if one is not careful. We can view the teasel's martial nature here as being more "clinging" than the thistle's, though less aggressive.

The teasel is one of many plants that have, in previous ages, been used to predict the weather. Hung in a place where air can freely pass through its body, the teasel was once said to predict coming cold snaps by its leaves, which would become smoother to the touch, and to predict coming rain by its prickles, which would slightly close.

Thistle

(Onopordon Acanthium, Carduus Lanceolotus, Carduus Nutans, and other species)

Folk names: *Scotch Thistle, Nodding Thistle, Spear Thistle, Musk Thistle, and others, depending on species*
Regions: Common in the British Isles, North America, and most other regions that experience freezing winters
Suggested Magical Uses: To Protect Against Enemies; To Curse the Enemy; To Divine Guidance

The general name *thistle* actually comprises a great variety of species, though with certain similar qualities, bearing striking purple flowers atop very tall stems and a prickly, thorny body that can be quite painful when touched accidentally. Its flowers develop and eventually disburse a great number of tufted seeds on the air. The folklore of the thistle is closely tied to these qualities of being thorned (defensive), tall (victorious), and prolific in its release of airborne seeds.

The thistle has been associated since ancient times with protecting against malefic spirits and entities. In Poland, the condition sometimes called "elf-lock" was believed to be remedied by burying thistle seeds. The variety referred to as *melancholy thistle* was once believed to protect from madness. The scotch thistle is said to have protected Scotland against an invasion of Norsemen in the 1300s. The men had removed their shoes in order to attack a sleeping town silently, but one warrior stepped on a thistle and cried out, alerting the people to wake and defend themselves against their attackers. The preservation of the image of the thistle in Scottish emblems is thus, in some ways, a culture-wide apotropaic talisman, a collective remembrance of this plant spirit's protective potencies.

On the other hand, the thistle is often associated with darker spirits and magics that are harmful rather than protective. In Germany, a thistle was said to grow once where a murder had been committed, and those who stumbled upon it accidentally could be stricken with paralysis. The darker associations with thistle are no doubt related to its painful prick and ubiquitous growth once it has made its home in a region, much to the annoyance of farmers.

The "milk thistle" or "Marian thistle" is an interesting exception here, since its white-spotted leaves are said to have been colored by Mary's milk as it fell from her breast. It is also sometimes called "Our Lady's thistle." It is more often included in medicinal herbals than other varieties of thistle, and has a long history of use in the healing arts.

Much like the dandelion, the wind-blown seeds of the thistle have been associated with divination and prophecy for many ages. Thistle seeds could either be blown in order to divine answers by the number of seeds remaining, or thistle flowers could be trimmed of their thorns and placed under the pillow to divine guidance. Unlike the use of dandelion tufts, which is sometimes associated with mortality and predicting deaths, the thistle's divinatory uses tend to be gentler in nature, having to do more often with love.

Thornapple

(Datura Stramonium)

Folk names: *Jimsonweed, Jamestown Weed, Devil's Trumpet, Devil's Weed, Devil's Snare, Moon Flower, Hell's Bells, Prickly Burr, Stinkweed*

Regions: Common in the British Isles, Continental Europe, North and South America, Asia, and many other regions

Suggested Magical Uses: To Exact a Wicked Curse Upon the Enemy; To Receive Dreams and Visions; To Open Gates Between Worlds; To Protect Oneself or Loved Ones from Harm; To Excite Tempers or to Calm Them; To Cause or Quell Madness

Thornapple or jimsonweed is an ancient plant that has been both venerated and villainized over the ages. It can grow quite tall, appearing in fields and places of disturbed earth with large leaves, great white and purple blooms that open to the moon at night, and its distinctly thorny seed pods. Its body emits a unique musky odor when bruised, resulting in its folk name *stinkweed*. Datura stramonium is lethally poisonous to the body, bringing terrifying mental delirium, heart failure, convulsions, and eventually death.

One famous bit of American folklore is related to its folk name *jimsonweed*, which is derivative of *Jamestown weed*. Reportedly, a group of soldiers in the historic Jamestown settlement ate the leaves of the plant, experiencing terrifying delirium in the aftermath. It is worth noting here that the term *hallucinogen* generally refers to substances that induce visual and auditory disturbances in the psyche. Thornapple is not a hallucinogen, but a *deliriant*. Its toxic effects are said to be universally horrifying and traumatic, often causing abusers of this plant to harm themselves or others involuntarily. In ancient times, it was known as *hippomanes*, causing horses who ate of it to go mad. While we would not seek the chemical actions of datura stramonium, its magical potency as a baneful herb makes it an ideal candidate for curse-work of a more wrathful and terrible nature than thistle or black nightshade, bringing the utter suffering and destruction of the enemy.

On the other hand, thornapple leaves were historically smoked as a treatment for asthma, and the plant was, in Culpepper's time, frequently used to ease spasms and inflammations, as well as to bring sleep. Needless to say, I do not recommend smoking or ingesting datura stramonium in any way. It is mentioned in early modern witch-lore as one of the herbs found in flying ointments, likely due to its narcotic properties. While I do not recommend working with datura stramonium directly for logical safety reasons, we must remember that the poison often lies not in the plant, but in its treatment, dosage, and manner of use.

In addition to otherworldly journeying and the opening of gates between worlds via the folkloric traditions of the witch's sabbat, thornapple has been used in Latin American cultures for many centuries to accomplish visions or prophecy of a more general nature, including for the location of hidden treasures.

That the thornapple possesses a strong lunar potency—in addition to the obvious saturnine influence at work in its poison—should be no surprise here. Its white, trumpet-shaped blooms are mesmerizing at night when they open to face the stars, drawing in moths, its favorite pollinators, by reflecting the soft glow of the moon hanging above. There is something entirely otherworldly about the blossoms of the thornapple, and the plant's spirit holds a recognizable kinship with witches, sorcerers, and charmers. In addition to its lunar and saturnine properties, thornapple has a very martial aspect discernable from its thorned seed pods. The plant is protective of its young, guarding what is most vulnerable with one hand while drawing in onlookers with the other hand by means of its ethereal beauty. Like the sorcerers who adore it, the thornapple is a complex spirit capable of both gentle aid and ruinous destruction, and the key to its magical nature lies at the fulcrum of this dichotomy, straddling both dextral and sinistral currents and the life and death they conjure.

Violet

(Viola Odorata, Viola Riviniana)

Folk names: *Wood Violet, English Violet, Garden Violet, Sweet Blue Violet, Dog Violet*
Regions: Common throughout the British Isles, the Americas, and Australia
Suggested Magical Uses: To Conceal Oneself or Others from Enemies; To Bring Love

Violet's most famous quality is the gentle fragrance of its flowers, which have for hundreds of years been used as a perfume ingredient and as a culinary one as well, the fresh flowers being made into jellies, syrups, and candies. Here we must differentiate between the sweet violet (viola odorata), which is scented, and the dog violet (viola riviniana), which is unscented, though no less beautiful. The greater part of the plant's folklore is likewise related to either the sweet scent or the vivid color of violet flowers, which have been associated with love and desire, but also with the qualities of concealment and secrecy. These qualities are embodied in the plant's tendency to go unnoticed due to its preference for shade and its short stature, being easily overlooked so low to the ground in its favorite shady patches.

The violet was prized in ancient times, even mentioned in legends as a perfume used by Aphrodite in order to win the adoration of Paris. Even hundreds of years ago, violet is noted as a "bridal flower" often included in the celebrations of marriage. In the spring (and sometimes autumn), the flowers of the violet are strikingly beautiful and fiercely colored, attracting early pollinators to partake of its sweetness. The heart-shaped leaves of the violet appear in the folk magical practices of many cultures, being pinned or sewn to clothing or simply carried to attract love and harmony.

This plant's Victorian associations with modesty are distilled in the common phrase "shrinking violet," used to refer to persons plagued by shyness. In actuality, the mythic origins of this association have less to do with shyness and more to do with arts of concealment for the sake of defense and protection. Its Greek name is supposedly derived from *Ion*, taken after the nymphs of the ancient region of Ionia. Myth tells us that Diana, goddess of the Moon, transformed one of her nymphs into the violet flower in order to help her escape the predatory pursuit of her brother, Apollo, god of the Sun. Alternately, legends say that Zeus transformed the priestess Io into the form of a cow in order to escape the wrath of Hera, and the first plant which sprung of its own accord to feed her was the violet.

In both of these tales, the violet embodies a potency of concealment that is sometimes necessary and useful, especially to those pursued by vengeful lovers and dangerous predators. These myths, as well as the violet's love of cool shade, were often interpreted in Victorian flower-lore to suggest a symbolism of modesty, shyness, and reserve. The violet's true potency in this aspect, however, lies in the concealment of what is beautiful and vulnerable for protective purposes.

Though the scented and unscented varieties of violet are sometimes confused, both are closely related and bear similar magical properties, though the sweet violet's uses are perhaps more potent in workings of an amorous nature than the dog violet.

Wood Sorrel

(Oxalis Acetosella, Oxalis Montana,
and related species)

Folk names: *Common Wood Sorrel, American Wood Sorrel, White Wood Sorrel, Hallelujah, Allaluia, St. Cecilia's Flower, Fairy Bells, Wood-Shamrock, Sleeping Beauty, Cuckoo's Meat, Cuckoo's Bread, Stickwort, Three-Leaved Grass, Sour Trefoil, Stubwort*

Regions: Common in the British Isles and North America

Suggested Magical Uses: To Perceive and Conjure Spirits; To Conceal One's Activities; To Find Joy Outside of Romance; To Bring Good Fortune; To Protect Against Harm

The wood sorrel's lore is somewhat mingled with that of the clover, but is distinct in a few unique aspects. Its physiology is interesting, for it is often noted as one of the "sleeping plants" that responds to levels of light and temperature. In the heat of the sun, its three-lobed leaves will come together to form pyramids, protecting it from too much water evaporation. In cooler, wet weather, the leaves fold flat against each other to shield the plant from frost.

Like the clover, the wood sorrel is often associated with Ireland

and other Celtic countries, as well as with St. Patrick. Moreover, it is similar to clover in its thorough associations with good luck, good fortune, and benediction (as opposed to malediction), for its form is often said to bear the trinity of the cross—said in older times to represent land, sea, and sky or pagan three-formed deities. It was also said to grow in the heavily wooded areas of ancient pagans before the coming of the church, and to grow especially thick in woods where they observed their rituals. Interestingly, wood sorrel is still noted today to prefer older, established forests, thriving in the presence of dense foliage and little sunlight. In Wales, the white flowers of the wood sorrel are sometimes called *fairy bells*, and they are believed to "ring" to summon the denizens of the otherworld to their revels during particular times. Wood sorrel is frequently associated with the workings of the fae in many currents of lore.

In the old *English Dictionary of Flowers*, the wood sorrel is noted as having the connotation of joy. It was in previous ages referred to as *hallelujah* or *alleluia* in many regions, including England, France, Spain, Italy, and even Germany, and this was said to allude to its blooming between Easter and Whitsunday. Since ancient times, the heart-like shape of its leaves was interpreted to denote preservation against many illnesses and diseases. It was reportedly once named "St. Cecilia's flower," a saint about whom many folktales abound. She is sometimes called the patron saint of musicians, for she sang hymns even while being forced to marry against her will. She is likewise related to "three-formed" symbolism, for she was said to have been struck three times across the neck with a sword, after which she survived for three days.

I view wood sorrel as a very lunar plant, being associated with the perception of otherworldly spirits, virginity, and revelry. This potency is also signaled three times over in its pale flowers, its dislike of the heat, and its love of darkness. Nonetheless, its heart-like form speaks to a certain venereal quality that feels more akin to a love of freedom or a delight in one's completeness unto oneself.

Wormwood

(Artemisia Absinthium)

Folk names: *Common Wormwood, Old Woman, Crown for a King, Madderwort, Smoke of our Lady, St. John's Belt, Guard Robe*
Regions: Common in Southern Europe, England, North Africa, and parts of North America
Suggested Magical Uses: To Divine the Future; To Bring Visions and Dreams; To Conjure Spirits; To Protect Against Evil Spirits; To Expel Unwanted Influences

Wormwood is closely related to mugwort (*artemisia vulgaris*), sharing some—but not all—of its magical properties and history of use. Like mugwort, wormwood is an *artemisia*, named after the goddess Artemis, and the herb is said to have been delivered by Artemis to the centaur god Chiron for use in his herbal craft. In ancient times, it was also said to have been carried by Egyptian priests during processions dedicated to the goddess Isis, another goddess associated with healing and magic. Like mugwort, wormwood has long been said to protect against evil spirits and dark magics. Because wormwood contains the toxin thujone, it is possibly harmful for some individuals, and internal use may be best avoided.

Whereas mugwort was once used as a flavoring agent in ale, wormwood has been used since ancient times as a flavoring for wine and spirits—more recently in the form of absinthe. The "green fairy" said to dwell within the absinthe is, in fact, the spirit of the wormwood itself, since it is the use of wormwood that defines traditional absinthe and delivers its mildly euphoric effects. This is most likely related to the presence of thujone in wormwood's composition, and it is for this reason a plant to take care with in regards to internal use, as it can result in some nasty side effects in certain individuals. Its association with euphoria and altered states of mind are also perhaps related to its use in divination and prophecy, for it was once said that an ointment prepared from Wormwood, if applied to the body while praying to St. Luke, would result in dreams of one's future fate. That wormwood is sometimes associated with necromancy is no surprise, since the altered consciousness that this herb is known for bringing is quite useful to various processes of spirit conjuration. This use is not without risk, as it is possible to poison oneself with wormwood.

Wormwood's protective properties are legendary to a degree even greater than its cousin mugwort. Like mugwort, it is sometimes associated with St. John, being identified as the belt or girdle that John the Baptist wore to protect him in the wilderness. Uniquely, though, wormwood was utilized in ancient disinfectant recipes, taken internally to expel worms and parasites, hung in the home to deter insects, and even placed in drawers alongside one's clothing to drive away moths. This use is the most likely origin of the name *guard robe*, derived from the French *garde robe*. Wormwood was even believed to be an antidote to all manner of poisons, including hemlock and the venom of serpents. Its ability to protect against wicked spirits was said to be even stronger when gathered on Midsummer Eve.

On the one hand, we can approach wormwood as another dreamy, visionary herb with clear lunar potencies, capable of transporting us to the otherworld or opening doors for spirits to make themselves known. On the other hand, its martial qualities are very well pronounced, even perhaps to a greater degree than mugwort, giving this herb an expulsive nature. It seems to not only protect the charmer, but actively assault and "drive out" unwanted influences in a very aggressive manner.

A Further Index of Plant Associations

While it is true that the Victorian language of flowers was used to express sentiments often difficult to convey in polite society, the old notion of the "language of plants" meant more than this. The Victorian years brought a great eruption of folklorists and folkloric preservation and scholarship, and with this movement, a strong interest in preserving popular wisdom and superstitions regarding not only the flowers available via the florist, but plants commonly found in gardens and in wild places. This preservation occurred, in part, through what we call the "language of flowers," which is, in fact, a distilled conveyance of a plant's history and associations of various kinds.

The following index of 208 plants is adapted from *The Language and Poetry of Flowers* (1877) as well as *Flora's Lexicon*: (1839). These keys enrich us by offering a small window into the historical associations of many plants, a foundation from which we can begin understanding a plant's nature. Rather than using this index simply as a prepackaged keyword list of magical associations, I recommend examining the plant more fully—both its physical form and its folklore and history—to try to understand *why* previous generations may have found that the plant's personality conveyed "deceit," "intellect," "prosperity," or "revenge." Taken at face value, these associations can block our path to a deeper understanding of plant spirits; taken as a clue, they can lead us deeper into the wood that lies before us, like a hand gesturing towards a hidden trail.

> Acacia – Friendship, Elegance, Secret Love
> Acanthus – Fine Arts, Artifice
> Acalia – Temperance
> Aconite – Misanthropy
> Aconite, Crowfoot – Lustre
> Agrimony – Thankfulness, Gratitude
> Allspice – Compassion
> Aloe – Grief, Rigidness
> Alyssum (Sweet) – Worth Beyond Beauty
> Amaranth (Globe) – Immortality, Unfading Love
> Amaranth (Cockscomb) – Superficiality, Affectation
> Amaryllis – Pride, Timidity, Splendid Beauty
> American Cowslip – Divine Beauty
> American Elm – Patriotism
> American Linden – Matrimony
> American Starwort – Welcome to a Stranger, Cheerfulness in Old Age
> Angelica – Inspiration
> Apple – Temptation, Preference, Fame
> Apple, Thorn – Deceitful Charms
> Apricot – Doubt

Ash Tree – Grandeur
Aspen Tree – Lamentation
Asphodel – My Regrets Follow You to the Grave
Bachelor's Buttons – Celibacy
Balm – Sympathy
Balm of Gilead – Cure, Relief
Balsam – Touch Me Not, Impatient Resolves
Barberry – Sourness of Temper
Basil – Hatred
Bay Leaf – I Change But in Death
Beech Tree – Prosperity
Belladonna – Silence
Betony – Surprise
Bindweed – Insinuation, Humility
Birch – Meekness
Birdsfoot Trefoil – Revenge
Bittersweet Nightshade – Truth
Black Poplar – Courage
Blackthorn – Difficulty
Bluebell – Constancy
Bramble – Lowliness, Envy, Remorse
Branch of Thorns – Severity, Rigor
Broom – Humility, Neatness
Burdock – Importunity, Touch Me Not
Buttercup – Ingratitude, Childishness
Butterfly Weed – Let Me Go

Cabbage – Profit
Cactus – Warmth
Camomile – Energy in Adversity
Cardamine – Paternal Error
Cedar – Strength
Cherry – Education
Chestnut – Do Me Justice, Luxury
Chickweed – Rendezvous
Chicory – Frugality
Chrysanthemum – Love, Truth
Cinquefoil – Maternal Affection
Clematis – Mental Beauty
Cloves – Dignity
Clover, Red – Industry
Clover, White – Think of Me
Coltsfoot – Justice Shall Be Done
Columbine – Folly
Coriander – Hidden Worth
Corn – Riches
Cowslip – Pensiveness, Winning Grace
Crocus – Abuse Not
Cypress – Death, Mourning
Daffodil – Reward
Dahlia – Instability
Daisy – Innocence
Dandelion – Rustic Oracle

Dead Leaves – Sadness
Dittany of Crete – Birth
Dock – Patience
Dogsbane – Deceit, Falsehood
Dogwood – Durability
Elder – Zealousness
Elm – Dignity
Enchanter's Nightshade – Witchcraft, Sorcery
Endive – Frugality
Everlasting – Never-Ceasing Remembrance
Fennel – Worthy of Praise, Strength
Fern – Fascination
Flax – Domestic Industry, Fate, I Feel Your Kindness
Foxglove – Insincerity
Fuller's Teasel – Misanthropy
Golden Rod – Precaution
Gooseberry – Anticipation
Grape, Wild – Charity
Grass – Submission, Utility
Hawthorn – Hope
Hazel – Reconciliation
Hellebore – Scandal, False Accusations
Hemlock – You Will Be My Death
Hemp – Fate
Henbane – Imperfection
Hibiscus – Delicate Beauty

Holly – Foresight
Honeysuckle – Generous and Devoted Affection
Hop – Injustice
Horse Chestnut – Luxury
Hyacinth – Sport, Game, Play
Hyssop – Cleanliness
Iris – Message
Ivy – Fidelity, Marriage
Jacob's Ladder – Come Down
Jasmine – Amiability
Juniper – Succor, Protection
Lady's Slipper – Capricious Beauty, Win Me
Laurel – Glory
Laurel, Mountain – Ambition
Lavender – Distrust
Lemon – Zest
Lettuce – Cold-Heartedness
Lichen – Dejection, Solitude
Lilac – First Emotions of Love
Lily, Day – Coquetry
Lily of the Valley – Return of Happiness
Liverwort – Confidence
Locust Tree – Elegance
Lotus – Eloquence
Magnolia – Love of Nature
Mallow – Mildness

Mandrake – Horror
Maple – Reserve
Marigold – Grief
Marjoram – Blushes
Meadowsweet – Uselessness
Milkwort – Hermitage
Mint – Virtue
Mistletoe – I Surmount Difficulties
Moonwort – Forgetfulness
Morning Glory – Affection
Moss – Maternal Love
Motherwort – Concealed Love
Mountain Ash – Prudence
Mouse-Eared Chickweed – Ingenuous Simplicity
Mugwort – Happiness
Mulberry Tree (Black) – I Shall Not Survive You
Mulberry Tree (White) – Wisdom
Mustard Seed – Indifference
Myrrh – Gladness
Myrtle – Love
Narcissus – Egotism
Nettle, Burning – Slander
Oak Tree – Hospitality
Oats – The Witching Soul of Music
Orange – Generosity
Ox-Eye – Patience

Pansy – Thoughts
Parsley – Festivity
Passion Flower – Religious Superstition
Peach – Unequaled Charms
Pear – Affection
Pennyroyal – Flee Away
Peony – Shame, Bashfulness
Peppermint – Warmth of Feeling
Pine – Pity
Plum – Fidelity
Pomegranate – Foolishness
Poplar, Black – Courage
Poplar, White – Time
Poppy, Red – Consolation
Poppy, White – Sleep, My Bane, My Antidote
Potato – Benevolence
Primrose – Early Youth
Purple Clover – Providence
Rhubarb – Advice
Rocket – Rivalry
Rose – Love
Rue – Disdain
Rush – Docility
Saffron – My Happiest Days Are Past
Sage – Domestic Virtue, Esteem
Saint John's Wort – Animosity, Superstition

Snapdragon – Presumption
Snowdrop – Hope
Sorrel, Wood – Joy
Spearmint – Warmth of Sentiment
Star of Bethlehem – Purity
Sunflower – Haughtiness
Sweet Basil – Good Wishes
Sweet William – Gallantry
Sycamore – Curiosity
Tansy, Wild – I Declare War Against You
Teasel – Misanthropy
Thistle – Austerity, Retaliation
Thornapple – Deceitful Charms
Thyme – Activity
Trefoil – Revenge
Truffle – Surprise
Tulip – Fame
Turnip – Charity
Valerian – An Accommodating Disposition
Venus' Trap – Deceit
Vervain – Enchantment
Vine – Intoxication
Violet – Modesty
Walnut – Intellect, Stratagem
Watermelon – Bulkiness
White Mullein – Good Nature

White Poplar – Time
Willow, Water – Freedom
Willow, Weeping – Mourning
Witch Hazel – A Spell
Wormwood – Absence
Yew – Sorrow

Epilogue:
The Black Meadow

Do *not walk in the wilds at night.* This has long been sensible advice. In the nocturnal wilderness, we are no longer creatures of mind and skill, able to outwit predators and exert control over the forces of nature, but are vulnerable prey, as fragile as any woodland creature hiding for survival. The wild dark reveals what we truly are: creatures of blood, bone, and flesh, no more or less important than the deer that keeps its careful vigil so as not to be made a meal by wolves.

And yet, the black meadow calls to us in our dreaming. Many are the tales of wanderers who stumble upon secret gatherings in the fields at night, sometimes never to return, or to return somehow changed by their encounter with the spirits of wild places and the secret rites they perform. All of us know a story like this; the creek where we do not walk for fear of seeing the ghost, the hill we avoid for fear of the creature said to dwell there, the pond where children will not swim, not after the farmer swore he saw that *thing* in the water. We are both terrified and hypnotized by the dark unknown, obsessed with dreaming about what may or may not dance among the trees at night.

For human beings, the pull of the dark is only natural. Its allure, we know on some level, lies in our desire to *see* with hidden eyes, to *feel* rather than intellectualize, to *step outside of ourselves*, shedding the narcissistic, futile human effort to master the wild, and to instead become wild again ourselves. We are like the deer, the wolf, the serpent winding into its tunnel at night. We, too, feel the call of the euphoric wisdom of instinct. *Mind the dark*, it tells us. *Keep your careful vigil. Something is always out there. You are not the master here.*

For witching folk, the black meadow's song means something else as well—that we, as the living generation of the long line of charmers who came before, are called to respect the sanctity of spirits, to not interrupt their peace, to not disturb their right to their own holy secrets. We may be *invited*, in moments of ritual, to drink from that dark well, and we may even, over time, earn the privilege of communion, but we may not intrude without their leave. The black meadow does not owe us its secrets. We are not entitled to sit at its feasting table. These things must be earned, and they must be offered, lest we incur wrath from ancient beings who mastered the art we treasure long before we were born.

The spirits we are discussing—and the gardens they tend so carefully—are described in our lore behind various veils and guises. There is the superstition of the Devil's acre, the small patch of one's farm that is allowed to grow wild in return for a good harvest. There is also the lore of the faery ring, which is a circle of fungal growth best left to its own devices. In Appalachia, there is the "laurel hell," a winding throng of growth that is best avoided, lest one become lost in its snarls. There is both beauty and darkness in these treasures of folklore, much like the field of Cain, which was made fertile by blood, but also gave way to life—Cain being the folkloric ancestor of some varieties of witching arts, said to have discovered the secrets of agriculture, the lunar calendar, and some of the ancient rites thereof.

This is to say nothing of the ancient spirit known as Hecate, appearing in many forms over the centuries, most recognizable as a dame of the wilderness, a lady of the crossroads. Though thoroughly associated with witchcraft and the spirits of the dead, she is also knowable—and has been since ancient times—as a patroness of wild places, forests and meadows beyond the boundaries of human settlement. Her territory is the unblemished wilderness, left to its own devices, allowed to keep its own balance. In her ancient rites, it was said that offerings left to her should be done in darkness, and that one should not look back after making the offering, but walk away quietly, with eyes turned. What would happen if we were to look upon her? Perhaps something like the fate that befell Actaeon, the hunter who dared to gaze upon the bathing Diana, and for this offense, was transformed into a stag and hunted by his own hounds.

When we respect the sanctity of spirits, their right to exist and to keep their own territories, we are robbed of nothing, and have a great deal to gain in terms of progress in our craft. The old rites of banishment and exorcism of so many "evil spirits" are, in many ways, rooted in our urge to subdue wild things, to bend nature to our will, to sanitize and impose our selfish designs upon what was here long before us. This urge expresses itself both spiritually and environmentally, for human beings have literally encroached on the wilds all over this planet, to such a degree that there is, in many places, nowhere left for them to dwell, no home of their own to be found. Deer wander down city streets after storms, for they can find nowhere else to flee. Bears travel into suburbs, stumbling into traffic in their confusion, robbed of the places where they once foraged and hunted for food. The media portrays the event as a horror, and in a way it is, for we have stolen *more than our share*, a crime that, in all of nature, only a human being is truly capable of, for we are the only creatures who evade the interdependence of nature's harmony, the only beings who take, but do not give.

Our task, then, as witching folk, is made harder. The road is more difficult, given the context of how humans have treated this world. How can we make the bond with these spirits who are our kin, knowing that we also belong to a tribe that has tormented, stolen, and killed for mere pleasure? Our spirits may be marked by the otherworld, but our bodies look exactly like betrayers, torturers, and destroyers of the sacred wild.

The answer, I feel, is this: with a radical love, and with a radical kindness—a kind of caretaking that is, paradoxically, also deeply instinctive to us, the neglected side of our nature. It is *natural* to feel satisfaction and joy when adopting a stray animal that would otherwise suffer needlessly. It is *natural* to feel fulfillment when planting trees and witnessing the wildflowers erupt from a patch of land that is allowed to once again become a meadow. It is *natural* to delight at the return of birds, butterflies, garden spiders, and moths when their food sources are restored. It is *natural* for the farmer to feel wonder at the birth of new livestock and to take pride in the well-being of animals, even if they are later to be slaughtered for food—a quick, clean death delivered by the hands that fed and cared for them, a death that stands in stark contrast to the drawn-out cruelty of industrial meat production. We are creatures of malice, but we are also creatures of empathy, capable of feeling what other beings feel, even if they look and act nothing like us, even if they are creatures of darkness, like the serpent, the spider, the bat, and the toad, all creatures of the witching kind in their own ways, and all with important roles to play. Something ingrained within our nature calls us to care for other beings, and when we fulfill this purpose, we are nourished.

When we can look on the black meadow with fear and love in equal measure, recognizing its right to exist alongside our own, we bring into balance two halves of our own nature, and we are better able to commune with and understand the spirits whose power we seek. Spirits are infamous in the lore of all cultures for their respect for fair deals, agreements, contracts, and pacts. This is the one "great pact," then, the pact that human beings have for too long denied: that all creatures have a purpose, that all living things deserve to exist, be they venomous or vulnerable, our predators or our prey.

I have wondered, at times, if there is a collective curse upon us. In our violation of this great pact of interdependence, in our hatred for the wild and the dark, we seem to be turning more and more upon each other. As we forget our natural, instinctive powers of empathy for other beings, so too are we losing our empathy for ourselves, for human kind. It is almost as if, in ill use of this gift, it is slowly being rescinded by some ancient power, some ancient collective of spirits, who are beginning to doubt our ability to fulfill our purpose as caretakers. Needless conflicts boil over all around us. Death and violence plague us. And still, we cannot see the irony, cannot answer the riddle before us, that we will never "cast out the evil," "defeat the enemy," or "conquer the darkness," for in the effort to subdue, purge, and destroy the other, we only wind tighter the cursing knot against ourselves.

The black meadow is both without and within. It is the dark behind our very eyelids, the shadow behind our own footsteps. We are creatures of darkness, dear reader, as surely as we are creatures of sunlight. We are blessed with a spirit that is tinged by shadow, every one of us, charmers all. We are instinctive and wild at our core, possessed of feeling and visions, full of the sweet, black nectar of the unknown and unknowable. The world we make around us is our dream, and we are dreaming together like the night-time forest, roots entangled with one another, breathing in the dark.

There is still time enough, I believe, for one more dream in this night of ours. Let us dream a good dream, then—one that relishes this beautiful and terrible garden, one that does not burn it down.

Bibliography and Further Reading

Arber, A. R. (1912). *Herbals: Their Origin and Evolution.*
Arsdall, A. V. (2010). *Medieval Herbal Remedies: The Old English Herbarium and Anglo-Saxon Medicine.*
Campbell, J. G. (1900). *Superstitions of the Highlands and Islands of Scotland.*
Carmichael, A. (1900). *Carmina Gadelica: Hymns and Incantations with Illustrative Notes on Words, Rites, and Customs, Dying and Obsolete: Orally Collected in the Highlands and Islands of Scotland.*
Child, F. J. (1904). *The English and Scottish Popular Ballads.*
Clavicula Salomonis. Historic Manuscript. (15th Century). Various Editions.
Cockayne, T. O. (1865). *Leechdoms, Wortcunning, and Starcraft of Early England: Being a Collection of Documents, for the Most Part Never Before Printed, Illustrating the History of Science in This Country Before the Norman Conquest.*
Coles, W. (1656). *The Art of Simpling.*
Culpeper, N. (1653). *The Complete Herbal.*
Dalyell, J. G. (1834). *The Darker Superstitions of Scotland, Illustrated from History and Practice.*
Davies, E. (1809). *The Mythologies and Rites of the British Druids.*

Deas, L. (1898). *Flower Favourites: Their Legends, Symbolism, and Significance.*

Dierbach, J. H. (1833). *Flora Mythologica oder Pflanzenkunde in Bezug auf Mythologie und Symbolik der Griechen und Romer.*

Dioscorides, P. (50 C.E.). *De Materia Medica.*

Folkard. R. (1884). *Plant Lore, Legends, and Lyrics: Embracing the Myths, Superstitions, Traditions, and Folk-Lore of the Plant Kingdom.*

Friend, H. (1886). *Flowers and Flower Lore.*

Gregor, W. (1891). "The Scotch Fisher Child." *Folk-Lore: A Quarterly Review of Myth, Tradition, Institution, & Custom.* Vol. 2.

Grieve, M. (1931). *A Modern Herbal.*

Grimorium Verum. Historic Manuscript. (19th Century). Various Editions.

Guazzo, F. M. (1608). *Compendium Maleficarum.*

Hardwick, C. (1872). *Traditions, Superstitions, and Folk-Lore (Chiefly Lancashire and the North of England).*

Hatsis, T. (2015). *The Witches' Ointment: The Secret History of Psychedelic Magic.*

Lacnunga ("Remedies"). Untitled Historic Manuscript. (10th Century). Various Editions.

Lemegeton Clavicula Salomonis. Historic Manuscript. (17th Century). Various Editions.

Le Petit Albert. Historic Manuscript. (18th Century). Various

Editions.

MacGregor, A. (1901). *Highland Superstitions Connected with the Druids, Fairies, Witchcraft, Second-Sight, Hallowe'en, Sacred Wells and Lochs, with Several Curious Instances of Highland Customs and Beliefs.*

Morley, M. W. (1899). *The Honey-Makers.*

"Names of Flowers." (1882). *The Cornhill Magazine.* Vol. 45.

Northcote, R. (1903). *The Book of Herbs.*

Scot, R. (1584). *The Discoverie of Witchcraft.*

Smith, W. (1846). *Dictionary of Greek and Roman Biography and Mythology.*

Taylor, B. (1900). *Storyology: Essays in Folk-Lore, Sea-Lore, and Plant-Lore.*

Thistleton-Dyer, T. F. (1889). *The Folk-Lore of Plants.*

Thorpe, B. (1852). *Northern Mythology: Comprising the Principal Popular Traditions of Scandinavia, North Germany, and the Netherlands.*

Warwick House. (1877). *The Language and Poetry of Flowers: With a Complete Vocabulary; Together with a Collection of Selected Poems.*

Waterman, C. H. (1839). *Flora's Lexicon: An Interpretation of the Language and Sentiment of Flowers.*

Wilby, E. (2006). *Cunning Folk and Familiar Spirits: Shamanic Visionary Traditions in Early Modern British Witchcraft and Magic.*

Wilby, E. (2010). *The Visions of Isobel Gowdie: Magic,*

Witchcraft, and Dark Shamanism in Seventeenth-Century Scotland.

Wirt, E. W. (1855). *Flora's Dictionary.*

Printed in Great Britain
by Amazon